LIFE IN FOUR CONTINENTS

Prakash Vinod Joshi

Gotham Books

30 N Gould St.
Ste. 20820, Sheridan, WY 82801
https://gothambooksinc.com/

Phone: 1 (307) 464-7800

© 2025 *Prakash Vinod Joshi*. All rights reserved.

No part of this book may be reproduced, stored in a retrieval system, or transmitted by any means without the written permission of the author.

Published by Gotham Books (April 11, 2025)

ISBN: 979-8-3485-8104-6 (H)
ISBN: 979-8-3484-9392-9 (P)
ISBN: 979-8-3484-9393-6 (E)

Because of the dynamic nature of the Internet, any web addresses or links contained in this book may have changed since publication and may no longer be valid.

The views expressed in this work are solely those of the author and do not necessarily reflect the views of the publisher, and the publisher hereby disclaims any responsibility for them.

Contents

PREFACE iii
Acknowledgements iv
The Early Days in East Africa 1
Back in India for a holiday 15
School Days in Uganda – Primary School 24
School Days in Uganda- High School 28
Kololo "A" Levels and Depart for England 49
Life in London and The Asian Exodus 60
Canada-Family Reunification 68
Career High and Break-Up 72
Mans' Best Friend-Kids and the Dog 83
My Wife – Darshana 90
The Family Grows 103
The historic visit of His Holiness the Dalai Lama 111
Native Chief Mercredi
Following Mahatma Gandhi's Non-Violence Way 116
Raj Mohan Gandhi Carries on The Legacy of His Grandfather 120
Farewell to Rev. Pandurang Shastri Athavale 121
David Suzuki - The Autobiography 126
Visit to Mt. Currie 132
India - Tibet has a Guru-Disciple relationship
His Holiness Dalai Lama 138
Reconciling Communities on Canada Day 145
UVIC Honours Miria Matembe of Uganda 150
Conclusion-Canada 155

Family and Friends – Later Years of Fond memories in photos	180
Work History in photos	201
Volunteer Work	206
Music- Special Fond Memories	212
Cricket - (IndCan Cricket Club of BC)	217

This book is dedicated with respect to Vinod and Indu Joshi, my parents Ronak, Tejaswini and Milan, my children, who helped me gaze into the future Darshana, my soul and best friend, who showed me the meaning of love and commitment.

Deer Lake Park
Found Peace

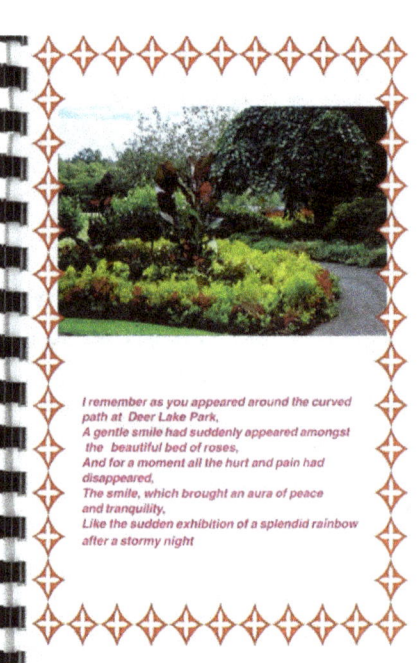

I remember as you appeared around the curved path at Deer Lake Park,
A gentle smile had suddenly appeared amongst the beautiful bed of roses,
And for a moment all the hurt and pain had disappeared,
The smile, which brought an aura of peace and tranquility,
Like the sudden exhibition of a splendid rainbow after a stormy night

PREFACE

As my parents were getting older, I felt the time was right to record the interesting and often challenging events that had crossed our paths. This would also be my contribution to my children if they ever wondered about their past. The journey that my grandparents started, from India to East Africa, with their early setbacks and settlements in unknown and often harsh environments, was most commendable and is often taken for granted by the newer generation. There was talk about Indians exploiting Africans. Yet, my maternal grandfather was known to visit an African leprosy village to help the sick and "forgotten Ugandans" and my paternal grandfather was known to open the shop door in the middle of the night to assist African customers by providing emergency supplies. This was our new home, Uganda, but soon we fell victim to a leader who had a different idea; he gave us three months to get out of the country. The family was split, some ended up in the United Kingdom, some returned to India, one uncle went to Brazil, while some of us landed in Canada.

"Life in Four Continents" describes this journey with a sense of humor, which is often needed when everything else seem to go awry, especially when strangers in a new country are ready to land a hand and so-called friends and family take advantage of you. I am proud of my new country, Canada; proud of my heritage, Indian; proud of the country of my birth, Uganda; but sad about the 500,000 Ugandans, mostly Africans, who perished at the hands of Idi Amin.

Acknowledgements

I am very grateful to my wife Darshana who persistently encouraged me to write this book, and all the poems are entirely dedicated to her and the love I have for this country Canada, this province of British Columbia and especially to the parks of this beautiful city of Vancouver.

Following my appeal for information, my parents' generous response after stretching their memories to the limit is most commendable. My love for my dear brother, Jyotindra, and his sense of humor has also helped me in the process of writing this book. I also thank my relations from as far away as East Africa (uncle: Ramesh Pandya), India (father-in-law: Major Krishnakant Vyas and cousin: Rajen Metha), and England (uncle: Rupshanker Joshi and Shirish Mehta) for providing me with the historical input and family information required.

My thanks to my friends Chris Hartnell and Jack Freebury who have assisted whenever they can to review my articles before they were published in newspapers or magazines.

My special thanks to the former editor and publisher, Pramod Puri, of the newspaper "The Link" and its current editor, Paul Dhillon, who have always supported my writings.

I am deeply thankful to our family friend and co-volunteer at "Initiatives of Change," Hilary Kariotis, for taking the time to edit "Life in Four Continents."

My inspiration for sharing my thoughts and my sincere desire to improve the situation of people and our "only" planet comes from "gurus" like Shree Morari Bapu, his Holiness the Dalai Lama, the late Swami Chinmayananda, the late Rev. Pandurang Shashtri Athvale, and not forgetting our popular Canadian environmentalist Dr. David Suzuki, all of whom I have had the privilege to meet.

The special role of some of my very dear friends like Neil & Nancy McAskill (Burnaby, BC), Roland Heere (Vancouver, BC), Dayabhai

Patel (Atlanta, USA), Greg Wilson (Coquitlam, BC), Arvind & Pratiksha Patel (Michigan, USA), Dineshbhai Patel (San Francisco, USA), Margaret Mubanda (Surrey, BC), Yutaka Hashimoto (Vancouver, BC), Dr. Cesar Chan (Illinois, USA), Raju & Divya Patel (London, U.K.), Sirishkumar Manji [Tabla Nawaz] (London, UK), Roy Naidu (Burnaby, BC), Sanjay Morar (Burnaby, BC), Pravin Shah (Burnaby, BC), Milton & Vallerie Carrasco (Richmond, BC), John Norohna (Toronto, Ontario), Azim Abdulha (Vancouver, BC), Yasmin Jamal (Karachi, Pakistan), Sachdev Singh Seyan (London, UK), Kalwant Singh Ajimal (London, UK), Dr. Dushyant Yagnik (Montreal, Quebec), Herman Desouza (London, UK), Peter Fernandez (Montreal, Quebec), Anwar Omar (Ottawa, Ontario), Dr. Virgil Dias (California, USA), Murari Dave (Burnaby, BC), the late Navin & Anila Tailor (Burnaby, BC), Vraj Sudra (Coquitlam, BC), Bob Gill (Vancouver, BC), Dr. Nemi Banthia (Vancouver, BC), Bhan Sinha (Burnaby, BC), Dr. Rajesh Desai (Coquitlam, BC), Kiran Patel (Burnaby, BC), Arvind Bhatt (Mumbai, India), Rahul Patel (Mumbai, India), Mohan Gandhi (Paris, France), Kesar Babra (Uppsala, Sweden), Avinash Kotecha (Viginia, USA), Punnag Hazarika (New York, USA), and plenty of others who have played an important role in my life to make this book worth writing. Many who were thrown far and wide, all over the world due to the exodus from Uganda, but who remain close to my heart.

Finally, I am grateful to National Geographic Magazine, to which I've subscribed since 1978, to help confirm some historical and geographical facts.

The Early Days in East Africa

In late 18th century Revashanker Joshi with his wife Dayaben departed from Patanvav (near Dhoraji) in the state of Gujarat in India to go to Africa. He was hired as an accountant by Alidina Vishram, a trading company. His journey must have taken him and his wife (my grandparents) a few weeks of travel by ship, from Porbandar (Costal town on the West coast of Gujarat on the Indian Ocean) to the East coast of Africa to a town called Mombasa. The route taken for hundreds of years by Indian traders using dhows.

(It was in 1948 that the Portuguese explorer with his four ships and a crew of one hundred and seventy men reached Port of Mombasa . He was the first European to sail around Africa to India. Here he met with Arab hostility and departed further North to a more friendlier Port called Malindi. Here, for the first time he noted the first sign of Indian traders. Gama and his crew contracted the services of an Indian pilot who had the knowledge of the monsoon winds which allowed him to bring the expedition to rest of the way to Calicut, located on the South West coast of India, South of now the famous Indian tourist resort of Goa)

From Mombasa they travelled by the recently built railway line, (Construction of the railway line started in 1896 from Mombasa and reached the Eastern shore of Lake Victoria, source of the great River Nile to a town called Port Florence, later named Kisumu in 1901). From Kisumu (in Kenya) a boat transferred them to a small town called Port Bell in Uganda. By 1931 the railway line was extended from Port Bell to the interior part of Uganda, now the capital city of Uganda, Kampala. The British had built the line, mainly with the help of sikh labourers to provide a modern transportation link to carry raw materials out of Ugandan colony and to carry manufactured British goods back in.

It was in a small town of Mpumu (another coastal town on Lake Victoria near Port Bell) that my father,

Vinod Joshi was born on September 8th 1928, youngest of the four siblings, eldest sister named Manglaben (Full name after marriage: Manglaben Mohanlal Shukla), and two brothers Labhshanker and

Rupshanker Joshi who both apparently worked for the East African Railways in later years.

My dad has fond memories of visiting his favourite uncle in a nearby small town called Gilgil where the Italian Prisoners of World War 1 were kept. The British later used them to build beautiful asphalt roads throughout East Africa.

Revashanker Joshi after leaving Alidina Vishram company opened his own shop in Buligami, near

Mpumu. From Buligami the brothers commuted by foot to the Old Kampala elementary and Senior Secondary school which was about seven miles away. My father remembers going to school with his good friend and neighbour, Mazar Ul' Haque taking this meandering path surrounded by tall elephant grass. It was at Bulimagi that the two elder brothers were thoroughly beaten up one day, by some Africans whilst coming back from school. Somabhai Patel a station master for Kampala Railways and also the cricket captain for Kampala Railways Cricket club liked Rupshanker Joshi, the middle brother as a cricket player and wanted him to play for his team and so not only did he recruit him in his team but also found him accommodation at Patidar Samaj Building on Kampala Road. Furthermore, gave him a job at the Railway Station. Later my dad joined the same club, too. Another tragic incident that suddenly took the family by surprise was the shop accidently go up in flames and caused my grandfather to move in with sons at a new location across the Railway Station called "Ashok Building". Labhshanker Joshi the eldest brother, joined the East African Railways, too but in Nairobi Kenya. My dad was only 12 years old when his father passed away at "Ashok Building" in 1940 and in a year later lost the mother (Dayaben) too.

It was in this early years that the true personality of my father, called "Natu" for short (Full name: Vinodrai Revashanker Mayaram Joshi) was developed and noticed by the whole family as the most bravest, fearless, adventurous child, able to bear extreme physical pain and most mischievous, and the incidences and the accidents that he got involved in, are still talked about by the extended family over and over again at family reunions. He loved animals and showed extreme kindness to people from various ethnic backgrounds.

Here are some of the incidences which are both tragic and at the same time painstackingly funny at times but portrays his true character build-up:

- He was hardly ten when after watching a Tarzan movie he decided to leap from a second storey building, landing in a ditch and totally fracturing his right arm. With a broken arm, literally hanging from the elbow and without a tear in his eyes, afraid of being scolded by the family he went to a Sikh family friend who helped in healing broken bones. He tried to quickly lock the bones together, rubbed some ointment and bandaged his arm. The healer was in complete shock when the child did not show any sign of pain. The damage caused by the compound fracture still remains as he cannot completely rotate his arm.

- Few of his uncles and aunt used to narrate an incident when my dad who was only about 13 years old decided to give some neighborhood kids a treat by giving them a ride in a truck. The whole bunch of them were ordered to pile up at the back and the driver released the brake and the truck rolled down the hill and crashed against a tree, little damage done to the truck but kids came out of the roller coast ride, unscathed.

- Realizing he was shorter than an average kid, he decided to do some pull-ups, hanging from a water pipe which ruptured and caused the house to flood.

- Always ready to give a helping hand, decided to give a friend a ride on his bicycle, after school, there was no rear sit so the friend stood at the rear with his feet on the stand mounted on the axis of the wheel on either side and his hands holding firmly on to dad's shoulder. They sped away down the hill. Suddenly dad realized a truck in front of him had come to a stop and was trying to turn at the intersection, he shouted and warned his friend to hold him tightly but it was too late. As he braked, he was in full control of the bike, just swirling a bit but the poor friend flew over his head and landed in the back of the truck, badly bruised but was safe.

- He was often found on top of trees, mango trees, climbing at great heights eating fresh fruits while the other family members- cousins and friends waited below for some left overs.

- Youth years brought demands of looking good, keeping extremely fit and challenges of body building. Being poor, meant weight lifting gear had to come by using ingenious methods- used railway wheels. Push-ups meant, waking up the young nephew at very odd early hours of the morning, making him sit on his back while dad went up and down with his exercises, often scolding the sleepy-eyed nephew to keep awake and warn him from falling off his back.

- He was often seeing bringing stray dogs home, removing each tick carefully giving them a bath and feeding them.

- As he grew older and acquired a bike he was regularly seen giving rides to poor commuters who sometimes waited for a long time for buses, seem to remember the old days when he had to walk several miles to school and work and didn't have money for travel. At one time he picked someone at the bus stop, thinking my dad was a very good bike-rider as the ride seemed fairly smooth, he relaxed and let go off the grip, holding the seat-bar. A few minutes later my father said, "please let me know where you want to get off". There was no reply from the rear. My dad quickly made a "U" turn looking for the passenger. He found him at the last road stop, brushing off dirt from his clothes. My dad said, "Come on Jump on the bike, what on the earth happened?". The guy replied, "Well, it was a stop sign, so I thought you'll completely stop but as there was no traffic, you paused and took off suddenly, and I fell off, thank you for the ride but please carry on I'll go by foot the rest of the way."

The Old Kampala Secondary School brought the best of my dad in sports, he played field hockey, soccer but excelled specially in cricket. My uncle Rupshanker Joshi and dad were automatic favourites for the selection of the school team. On week-ends my dad was often seen on his bicycle, or on the sports ground or swimming at Kabaka lake, (This is the largest excavated lake in Africa. This lake was dug out on the orders of the king of Buganda called Kabaka Mwanga in the 1880's as an 'escape corridor' to Lake Victoria, but the actual link to the big lake was never achieved as he was driven from his capital by muslim dissenters.). Too many lives had been lost at this lake due to its swampy floor bed but that did not stop him from jumping in and spending a lot of time there and resulting him to be an outstanding swimmer.

In 1947 Labhshanker Joshi, dad's elder brother moved to Nairobi, Kenya to work with the Railways. Thinking that dad also could join the Railways after completing high school, or join the police academy if he wished, the brothers encouraged him to join him. Dad enrolled at the Duke of Glouster Senior Secondary School in Nairobi where he met Suryakant Patel who would turn out to be one of his best loyal long-time friends and play an important role in his life. He spend only one year in Nairobi but had the opportunity of being the youngest cricket players to represent "Kenya Railways Cricket Club". Climbing the Mt. Longonot which is located 60 kilometers southeast of Lake Naivasha, in the great Rift Valley with Suryakant Patel and his friends is another fond memories he cherishes. Mount Longonot is a dormant volcano, thought to have erupted in the 1860's with the highest peak at 2780 m. Its name is derived from the Masai word oloonon'ot, meaning "mountainsof many spurs" or "steep ridges".The mountain is home to beautiful specious of wildlife, notably hartebeest,Zebra, giraffe and buffaloes. Leopards have also been seen but at very rare occasions.

Back in Kampala, he landed a job with "Shell oil company" as a clerk, worked there for only six months and moved to then the capital of Uganda, Entebbe, known for its beautiful botanical gardens, white sandy beaches with the popular tropical zoo. This was a very popular picnic spot especially for Asians who sometimes came in bus loads from Kampala, about 20 miles from Entebbe. The international Airport at Entebbe was made famous by the movie "The Raid at Entebbe" which dramatized the actual freeing of hostages taken by Palestinian terrorists and supporters on Air France and taken to Entebbe Airport. The daring rescue called "Operation Thunderbolt" was conducted by the Israeli Defense Forces (IDF) on July 4, 1976. Idi Amin, the self- proclaimed president of Uganda who had overthrown the First democratically elected Prime Minister of Uganda, Milton Obote in a bloody coup, in 1971, claimed to negotiate the release of the hostages was seen more of a sympathizer towards the terrorists. This was obvious when after the Israeli raid he had one of the elderly Israeli hostages, Mrs. Dora Bloch who had been taken to the local hospital, (Mulago Hospital) for treatment murdered by his henchmen and the body thrown in middle of a sugarcane farm.

My father shared a room with a cricketer called" Rana", at Entebbe. They lived behind a shop owned by a gentleman called Parbat Harbham. He worked at the Uganda Medical headquarters as a correspondent between different heads of the ministry.

As a cricketer he was often invited at the residence of the acting British Governor General of Uganda, Governor John Wild who himself was a fond cricketer and would later represent Uganda 11 with my dad in 1957. Goven. John Wild and Dr. Macadam had recently visited England and learnt about "swing bowling" and introduced it to the Ugandan players. The Ugandan team consisted mainly of British players, few Indians, amongst which was my dad, the youngest player in the team plus only one African, Prince Muwanda, brother of late king of Buganda, Kabaka Fredrick Walugembe Muteesa II.

Dad remembers how the selection of the Ugandan Team took place. Players came from all over Uganda for a friendly game at Entebbe where players were going to be selected based on their performance. Dad was not chosen as one of the twenty-two players. I asked dad and his reply was, "Politics, I did not come from a very strong community, Brahmin community was not as strong and

1951-Top photo shows player selection day. Bottom Photo shows selected Uganda Cricket Team

influencial as the strong Gujarati communities of the Patels, Shahs and the Lohanas. I came from a poor family, too. Plus the other Indian communities, Ismailis, Sikhs and Muslims backed their own players. The British had their own favourites." He was informed by a friend from the Goan community, Leo Gamma a cricket enthusiast and umpiring the game who asked my dad to come and bring his kit along, in case some players couldn't make it. This is exactly what happened, they were short. There was a bowling side, Captained by Governor General John Wild with Dr. Macadam, two good bowlers and there was the batting side. My dad was given an option and chose the batting side and scored 96 runs. He was selected.

As most of the family resided in Kampala, my dad decided to move back to Kampala but he needed a referral and a job in Kampala. The Governor General came to his aid by hooking him up with Uganda Post office. With a steady job, a motor-bike and a flat to live in, given by the Post office, it was time to settle down and look for a wife.

Porbander, a coastal town on the west cost of Gujarat is well-known. It is connected with Gandhiji's early childhood days. Ranavav is about an hours train ride, east of Porbander. I remember visiting this sleepy town when I was only seven years old with my brother Jyotindra who was six. "Bapa" had our full attention as he kept us entertained with true stories about the village. He would tell us about how he caught snakes with his bare hands or spotting tigers on the outskirts of the village. Then there was this swamy/monk who lived to about 100 years but spending most of his life in this cave. We had to see the cave and "Bapa" gave into our demands to see it and the swamy,too. Next day we jumped on to a horse carriage and aheaded towards the forest to see the" Jam buvan cave". As we descended into the cave, it was pitch dark, "Bapa" lighted a lamp and there was the swamy, sitting in the lotus position, hardly wearing any clothes greening and greeting us.

"Bapa" (Rupshanker Metha who lived with "Ba", Dayaben) was the elder brother of our maternal grandfather, Ishvarlal Metha who in the year 1924 left the village of Ranavav to go to Africa, taking a steamer from Porbander, crossing the Indian Ocean to Mombasa (Visiting his younger sister(Lalita Mehta who had married to a Headmaster of a local school, Mohanlal Pandya) then proceeding by rail to Kisumu on the shores of Lake Victoria, then taking a boat from there to Port Bell. From

Port Bell to Lugazi, his final destination would have been by road. The road journey would have taken him first to Kampala then travelling east through the dense tropical forest called" Mabira Jungle" and then finally reaching Lugazi. He would have seen a sudden clearing and a tea plantation. This was known as Nanji Kalidas Tea Estate (Gujarati Industralist) where he was appointed plantation manager and later Chief Manager at Kasaku Tea Estate. The promotion would have meant an improvement in living conditions from a corrugated tin housing to a concrete one. The tea estate had Indian staff employed as managers, accountants and technicians with African labour force. In

later years he moved to Lolgorian Gold mine, located at the border of Kenya and Tanzania. Grandpa recalled the area full of wild life, elephants, lions and wild buffaloes. The owners of the gold mine were Indians (Gujarati Lohanas) Kanji Naranji & brothers. My grandfather was often seen stomping the area with his white British colonial hat. There after he went back to Lugazi again to manage the tea estate. It was at Kasaku Tea Estate that my mother (Indumati Mehta) tied the wedding knot with my father (Vinod Joshi) on December 14th, 1949. The wedding was a simple event except for the bridegroom's car getting stuck in the muddy gravel road and the family and friends with theirfancy clothes were seen pushing the car to get it out of the ditch. The only entertainment consisted of an old Gramaphone with a trademark logo showing a dog listening to "His Masters Voice- HMV" through a trumpet. But there was only one record and so the dog and the guests at the wedding heard the same song ("Meh tehra chand tu mehri chandni"- I am your moon and you are my moonlight) again and again, whole daylong. The only difference was when the torque lessened on the gramophone, thereby reducing the speed of the turntable and the song slowed down then somebody had to run and turn the lever again to start the turntable to rotate again and the song resumed its normal speed again.

My dad was warned to stay put before the wedding day by his elder brothers. As he stood in the doorway of his house in Kampala, his best Sadar friend came around the corner with a newly purchased "Harley Davidson". The friend asked him to try it out. Dad couldn't refuse the offer, he simply loved bikes, the generous Sadar asked him to go all the way to Entebbe (35 miles) and come back to really feel the bike. On the way back he saw an African pedestrian walking along the side of the road but seemed a little drunk, as he approached the person, the pedestrian suddenly lost balance and fell right in front of the bike. He quickly steered away from the pedestrian to save his life but lost control and crashed. The bike was totaled, dad was bruised badly, one day before the wedding.

Special sitting arrangement were made for him to sit on a stool as he was so badly hurt that he couldn't fold his legs and sit on the floor as usually was the custom during a typical Indian wedding in those days. He continuously sighed, moaned and struggled throughout the wedding while my mother wondered and worried whether this was a forced wedding on his part.

My mother (Indumati Mehta) was born in Lugazi, Uganda on August 8th, 1931. She was the eldest of the three siblings with two brothers named Harshad and Shirish Mehta. The family lived happily for a while until the sudden death of her mother, Vijyagauri in 1936. Mom was only six years old when she had the additional responsibility of helping to look after the two younger brothers. When mom was just seven the grandfather had no choice but to go back to Ranavav, India to have his elder brother and wife look after the three kids while he returned to Lugazi to carry on working at the tea estate to financially support the family. He often made trips back to Ranavav, bringing gifts for the kids. He never married again and turned towards living a very religious life, waking up very early in the morning every day and reciting prayers for two hours from the holy Hindu book, "Geeta". He was known to be very kind to all, Africans, Indians and a few Britishers whom he encountered. This early morning ritual with the breathing yoga exercises called "Prayanama" continued until he passed away in 1971 in a small town of Masaka, North of Kampala where my brother (Jyotindra) and I used to visit him often during school holidays when we were young.

Growing up in Ranavav was extremely tough for my mother, she tirelessly worked long hours carrying out house hold chores plus working hard on the farm, carrying her baby brother who was hardly a year old on her back. Mom often mentioned about being so poor that she had only one

yellow sari to wear which she washed every evening after working, let it dry overnight and wear it again the next day. Times were a little better when she went to a slightly bigger city called Vadodara at the age of eight and started elementary school. She lived with her cousin (Dugabhai

Metha) who was married and had a good job. At the age of seventeen my grandfather decided to move her back to Mombasa and live with her aunt and soon after came the wedding proposal for her. This was going to be an arranged marriage, as was the custom during those days. The parents on either side after looking at the horoscope with consultation with a proper Brahmin priest had decided they were a good match. My dad came all the way from Kampala, Uganda (900 miles) to Mombasa, Kenya to look at the potential bride and the mother had the same right to look at the potential bridegroom and of course they both had the liberty to reject. As my dad sat in the living room, my mother came to serve him some snacks, they both had a look at each other, that was enough. Both fell in love with each other. But there was one big dilemma. Mothers' cousins had spread teasingly some rumours that "to be" bridegroom was shorter than her. This was grounds for total refusal for the marriage on my mother's side. She spent a sleepless night and worried about how to get to the bottom of the truth. My dad had resided at the same house, as soon as my dad got out of the early morning shower, my mother jumped in after and measured his pyjama hanging on the towel rack- "ha!" he was much taller, the cousins had all been lying, marriage proposal excepted. Now for the wedding in Kasaku in Uganda. (On January 14th, 2007 the family threw a surprise 50th wedding anniversary party for my parents in Vancouver, BC Canada, inviting about three hundred people, initiated and organized by my wife Darshana with help from our children, sons Ronak and Milan and daughter Tejaswini. The "surprise" overseas guests included my brother Jyoti, his wife Susan and daughters, Neesha and Neemisha from London, England. Mom's elder brother Harshad Metha and his wife Kusum came from Sao Paol, Brazil. Younger brother, Shirish Metha and his wife Ramila flew over from London, England.)

Living in Kampala with Uganda being a British Colony during 1950's, most of the Indians would have considered themselves lucky to be in one of the safest and most beautiful city to spend their entire life in. Winston Churchill called Uganda "The Pearl of Africa". Kampala features a tropical wet and dry climate, however due to city's higher altitude, the average temperatures are noticeably cooler than what is typically seen in other cities with this type of climate. Kampala is said to be built on seven hills. Mutesa 1, the Kabaka(king) of Buganda had chosen this area that was to become Kampala as one of his favourite hunting grounds. It was an ideal breeding ground for various game. Buganda is one of the oldest kingdoms in Africa, dating back to the late 13th century. With numerous lakes surrounding Kampala and with tropical fertile soil, fruits were plentiful and soon the Indians invested their time and energies on developing farms. tea, coffee, cotton, sugar-cane, just to name a few. Kampala became a modern city, very well planned and clean. It was in one of the suburbs called Kololo that we spend most of our lives before being kicked out of our country of birth, Uganda in 1971 by Idi Amin.

I was born in Kampala on October 10th 1950 followed by my brother on February 22, 1952. I was enrolled in a primary girl's school at first, called "Arya Girls School, the only reason being, it was the nearest school, available. I loved my brother the most and remember bringing mogo (cassava) chips for him from school. Being very protective of him, I was often seen picking fights with others, even with elders who tried to bully him or scold him. The only person who had the right to beat him up was me. My brother and I had long hair as it was a Brahmin tradition to have them cut in India after an elaborate religious ceremony.

Vinod Joshi *Indu Joshi*

Vijyagauri Mehta *Ishvarial Mehta*
(Parent of Indumati Joshi)

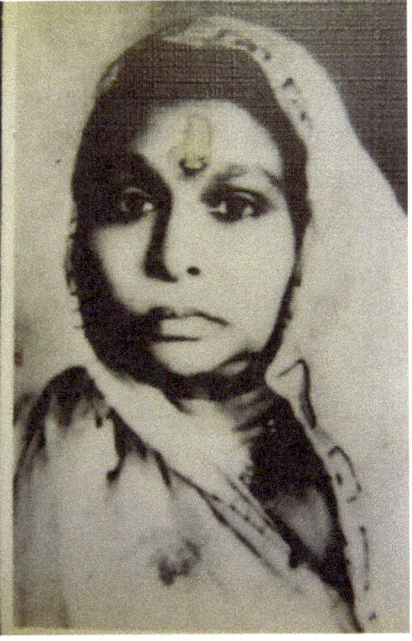

Revashanker Mayaram Joshi *Dayaben Joshi*
(Parents of Vinod Joshi)

**Shores of Indian Arm
Barnet Beach Park**

Like the waves racing towards the shore of the Indian Arm,
I race the world to see you one more time
Like a deserted dhow carried by
the wind wherever it pleases,
I go blindly to where my heart desires
And when I meet you at the lighthouse,
I would recite this poem to you,
Simple thoughts into words,
Which day-in, day-out linger in my mind for you.

BACK IN INDIA FOR A HOLIDAY

Dad was able to accumulate holidays at the Post Office so our trip to India usually lasted four or five months. The first time we visited we were too young to remember much except both of us brothers were not very happy suddenly loosing our long hair and being completely bald. I was only four and remember seeing the Taj Mahal at Agra and playing cricket with my favourite cousin, Rajen Metha in Vadodara. On night, while sitting behind a bicycle with my dad in front, riding it, I was suddenly stung by a scorpion on my leg, now that pain I still remember. As they say, "Seeing stars during day time", the true meaning I did appreciate on that particular day.

The second trip to India lasted about five months. I was just eight years old and it was most memorable. The train ride from Kampala to Mombasa with a stop at Nairobi was simply breath taking for even kids like us who were most of the time too busy running between compartments, sticking our heads out of the window taking in the cool breeze and seeing at a distance, the roaring and whistling of the steam engine ahead. But I do remember a few things. As we left Kampala, soon after an hours ride, the landscape suddenly changed we entered the thick dense Mabira forest, parents making a comment of not seeing even a few feet deep through it. Next seeing the Owen Falls Dam at the second biggest Industrial town of Jinja in Uganda. First was Kampala. (*The Owen Falls dam was built by the British in 1954 at the source of River Nile at Lake Victoria, providing electricity to most parts of Uganda and partly to Kenya). As we crossed the Uganda/ Kenya border the landscape changed to less vegetation and noticed more farms. Remembering going over wooden truss railway bridges and the rattling sound and thinking what would happen if the train would suddenly tip over. Rift Valley (The Great Rift Valley extends from Lebanon in the North to Mozambique in the South, in Kenya the valley is deepest North of Nairobi. The Rift Valley in East Africa has been rich source of fossils that allow study of human evolution) crossing was another site that comes to mind with meandering tracks going through the high mountains and tunnels and the vast open space/valley below with Kikuyu farms and mud huts. The Kikyu children waving at us, seeing for the first time, Kikuyu mothers carrying heavy loads on their backs tied with a strap going over their heads and the big ear rings which tore through the ear lobes and expanded them and the shiny metallic bracelets with colourful beads and the fancy-colored necklace with beads plus beautiful white smile. I remember a water falls and made the connection several years later that it was the "Thicka Water Falls" we had witnessed.

(*John Hanning Speke the great explorer, in 1859 thought he had resolved one of the greatest mysteries of the 19th century geography when he claimed Lake Victoria to be the source of River Nile. What he didn't know was that for the Nile to be the longest river in the world, the longest tributary leading into Lake Victoria from the south had to be added to its length. The National Geographic Society has traditionally recognized two sources of the Nile, one in Rwanda and one and one in Burundi, farther south. In case of the Nile, as with the Amazon, the enormity and complexity of the river system makes the use of the term 'source' a troublesome issue)

Top: Jyoti & Prakash / Middle: Ronak & Milan / Prakash & Jyoti

At Nairobi (Capital City of Kenya and has moderate climate due to its nearly 6000 feet altitude.

Location of the Nairobi railway camp was chosen due to its central position between Mombasa and

Kampala.) the weather turned slightly cold and there at the railway platform was my uncle

(Rupshanker Joshi and his wife Wimlaben) and at home cousins (Brothers Rashmi , the twins Niru/Nilesh and sisters Veena and Neetu.) eagerly waiting to greet us. Few years later I would hear of some very tragic news about my cousins loosing their loving mother, brutaly murdered by their own African servants, a case which took several years to solve but the culprits were caught. After a short stay in Nairobi the journey continued towards Mombasa by train. As we approached the market town of Voi with the semi-arid vegetation, we noticed, for the first time the sisal estates. We learnt that sisal yielded stiff fiber traditionally used in making twine, rope and dart boards. Voi was situated on the edge of the Tsavo National Park. I remembered my grandfather, Ishvarlal Metha the only surviving grandparent we brothers had ever met and known, telling us the horror stories of the pair of notorious man – eating lions responsible for the deaths of more than hundred Indian railway construction workers during the building of wooden railway bridge over Tsavo River. Two maneless males, huge Tsavo lions stalked the campsite, dragging Indian workers from their tents at night and devouring them. Crews tried to scare off the lions and built campfires through and bomas of thorn fences around their camp for the protection to keep the maneaters out, to no avail. The lions crawled through the thorn fences. Finally they were shot by an American hunter. As we left Voi, taking the final lap towards Mombasa we brothers couldn't help but think of the dreaded beasts as we slept on our favourite top bunkers and the train rocked to and fro on the tracks.

As we reached Mombasa, the dry coastal climate actually suited me very much as the constant sneezing in the morning had suddenly stopped. I fell in love with the town, though so young I still could remember every little detail and continued visiting the town as I grew older. The swaying palm trees, the shinny white sandy beaches, swimming in the Indian Ocean, taking a ferry on the way to Malindi, for hours starring at the

Arab dhows, visiting the lighthouse and finally playing around Fort Jesus, acting like "Famous Five", characters and their adventures from the popular children novels by famous English author, Enid Blyton. (Fort Jesus was built in 1593 by the order of king Phlips II, then ruler of the joint Portuguese and Spanish kingdoms. It was designed by an Italian architect in a shape of a man, located on Mombasa Island, it was built to guard the old Port of Mombasa, Kenya).

After a brief stay at Mombasa we were ready to cross the Indian Ocean on a ship" Karanza" which would first take us to Seychelles, a brief stop at the Islands of Seychelles, 480 km East of Mombasa and then on to Mumbai. The whole journey would take about two weeks. There was always something to do on the deck for us kids, play cards, run around play catch, play hide n'seek, look at the flying fish following the ship, occasionally see dolphins, make friends, food was plenty full and at night lying on the deck gazing at the stars and see movies. Weather was perfect. The ship was full of mostly Indian passengers, getting along well with each other, often travelling by ship as it was the best affordable way. As they spoke, it seems they always made connection with someone they

mutually knew. As we docked at Mumbai, I made an observation, the crows here were totally black compared to the ones in Uganda which had a bright white stripe on their back.

In Mumbai or Bombay as it was called then, parents managed to see the actual shooting of a movie called "Ganga jamuna", starring the popular actor Dilip Kumar and had our photo taken with him. I actually remember seeing that movie in Kampala and appreciated more visiting and touring the studio in Mumbai. The name "Bollywood" was not common as yet.

Next stop by train was Vadodara and remember visiting the Kamati Baag (Park), swaying on the suspension bridge, having an elephant ride and visiting the zoo. My cousin Rajen Metha and we brothers had the best time of our lives and to this date have one of the closest relation. We spent a lot of time at Vadodara, the highlight was the festival of" Utaraan", flying kites. Preparing for this festival meant making kites, applying glue with powdered glass on to the string used for flying kites.

This would assist in cutting the string of others who dared to come anywhere near your kite. This needed special skills. The sky would fill up with beautiful colored kites and as night approached lanterns were cleverly manoeuvred up the sky, hanging on the string of the flying kite. The roof tops would be filled with people, flying kites with popular Indian music, blaring from speakers. It was common to see monkeys jumping from one to roof to the other, they were part of the entertainment, begging for food. Rajen and family were poor in those days, livelihood depended on preparing and selling incense sticks. We would join in helping to make them. At night we would quietly sit in the balcony holding a string with a rag tied at the other end, thrown over the electric lines and as a unsuspecting passerby, especially smoking a "bidi" (cigarette) came along we would let the rag drop on his head. The reaction of the passerby would be so funny that we could not hold our laughter and sometimes got caught red handed but were always forgiven for our mischief.

As most of the time was spend in Vadodra and used as our central location, mom made sure that a tutor was hired if we had an extended stay so that our studies were not affected. What I fond amazing at that early age, how my cousins in India were so good at math and with strict discipline remembered math tables by practicing and memorizing them every day. My brother and I had a hard time coming anywhere close to the speed at which they could come up with the right answer. Boy! This Indians were good at math.

In Kololo we had a neighbor called Manohar Singh Sandhu and his wife Satwant Kaur. Manhor Singh Sandhu worked with Uganda Police (He later joined "Scotland Yard" in London, England after having to flee Uganda in 1971) who had one son (Pale') and two daughters Jiti (Inderjeet) and Gogi . The families became the best of the friends and on the day of "Raksha Bandhan ", usually Jiti would come around to tie "Rakhi" on us brothers on our right hands. (*Rakhi is basically a sacred thread of protection embellished with love and affection of sister for brother. This day is known as Raksha Bandhan. This frail of thread of Rakhi is considered as stronger than iron as it binds the beautiful*

relationship in an inseparable bond of love and trust. This day was special for us brothers as we didn't have any sisters. But sometimes I wonder whether it was uncles' idea of keeping his beautiful daughters away from my handsome brother. Pale is now in London, England working as an architect and Jiti is a physician married to my class-mate at Kololo Senior Secondary School, Tejinder Singh Hunz.

At this time Manhor Singh Sandhu, with his family was going to be in his village called Saneval (a farming community in Punjab). Saneval was close to the big industrial city of Ludhiana and have

Presently merged. He invited us to visit the farm house, predominantly a sikh town and the community had never seen a gentleman without a turban until my dad suddenly appeared from nowhere.

The ever-green fields of Saneval, water tube wells with gushing water running through the channels for irrigation, rides on the buffaloes, drinking fresh milk, eating homemade "naan" and tasty spiced vegetables of all kinds "sabji" come to mind. A day trip to Amritsar to see the biggest temple, The Golden Temple was a moving experience. What the young innocent eyes saw was a majestic shrine surrounded with water and copying the elders, joined their hands together, tipped their heads, touched the holy water to their foreheads.

From Ludhiana we headed further North towards Kashmir in a bus, and as we came closer to the famous mountain ranges of Himalayas the ride which I would remember the rest of my life as if it happened just yesterday became a night-mare. The narrow, winding roads were most treacherous, hats off to the bus driver, how cleverly he maneuvered the bus, sometimes an inch apart from the oncoming bus. Holding to our sit tightly at all times as the bus geared off right to the edge of the steep slope. Several vehicles which seems to have lost control could be seen at the bottom of the valleys. I remember going through a water falls, not seeing what was on the other side. As we approached Srinagar we felt the cold and were definitely not dressed for winter. We spent the first night in a motel and then moved to a "House Boat" on Lake Dal. But first, something had to be done about this chilling cold. This was the first time we had seen snow and experienced such weather and soon we were making preparation to go up to the ski resort called Gulmarg. We purchased Kashmiri shawls and clay fire pots called "manann". "mannam "with hot charcoal in it is held inside the shawl to keep warm and requires little practice, holding it and walking especially with your both hands inside the shawl. I got burnt slightly one day as I tried to hold on to the pot with one hand and tried to jump on a horse carriage holding on to the handle on the carriage, the horse moved, I lost my balance, and lost the pot too, got burnt a little but not much to warrant first-aid, there was plenty of snow around. Going up the mountain to Gulmarg was fun. Half way up was on a horse back and the rest we were pulled up on sledges for a reasonable fee. Mom had the biggest horse and didn't have fun riding it as he had a mind of his own or was it a "she", at every little water stream it would suddenly stop and bend over to take a drink, thrusting mum making her scream.

Our Kashmiri guide who was both extremely polite and honest and was most helpful from the time we got off the bus to having taken us around the key places including shopping for famous Kashmir wooden handicrafts, lamps, stools, carpets etc. A quick photo shoot on the top and we were back at the house boat. As papa and mummy took a nap, we two brothers took off on a canoe which was tied to the house boat used for taking tourists to and from the mainland to the house boat. Well, after a little hard work we both realized the rowing was not working and we were moving pretty fast by some water current in one direction. Soon we were quite a distance from the houseboat whenwe heard some people shouting at us from some a passerby canoes, we were actually heading to words some rapids or was it a water fall, we never found out as we were soon rescued and then came the scolding, we were getting quite used to getting into trouble.

Back at Vadodara, Dad had made sure that he had put a side time to participate in his two favourite hobbies, one playing cricket with his newly made friends. He played a game with "Hujarat Cricket Club" and has a proof to show for, "a team photo". His love for Indian music and naturally having a gift of a good singing voice meant he had to meet a few Indian musicians and have a music singing sessions with them. At Mumbai, Dad purchased a harmonium from "Haribhav Musical Instruments". This piece of antique beautiful wooden instrument with German rids has been with the family for nearly 53 years. The harmonium and an album of family photographs seem to be the only valuable items that I was able to take along with me when I fled Uganda at the age of 22 years. Everything else that we owned stayed behind.

On our return back to Uganda from India in 1958, we did not realize that we wouldn't be able to return to the country of our ancestors for the next nearly thirty years.

School Days in Uganda – Primary School

After a lot of complains I was transferred from the girls school to a co-ed school called Demonstration Primary school in the subbarb of Shimoni. Jyoti (Short name for Jyotindra for my brother) followed me, a year behind and seem to adjust to school faster than me. I was a slow learner but worked hard while Jyoti picked up studies faster in class. While he was constantly reminded about studies, I never had to be told. While I studied, he wanted to play and would annoy me by touching me and disturbing me, he kept it up until he heard the grinding of my teeth and then he would suddenly disappear. Girls found him extremely cute. While I faired better at sports he was good in plays/drama. Our school was about five miles from our home so in the morning we got dropped off in a car at school by dad but usually walked back home after school. It was my job to look after him and protect him while we were on our own.

I was extremely shy and never uttered a single word in class. It was in Grade 7 that thing changed. I saw a girl who started taking interest in me. In the class I was once forced to stand-up and answer a question, no teacher had dared to do that to me before, I was so afraid I broke down and started crying. The whole class laughed including the girl who had being eying me the last few days. That was too much for me to handle and the very next day I was a "new man". The other thing that helped me build up my confidence was the personal tutor, (Hilary Da' Silva) who my parents had hired and came down on his scooter three times a week to teach my brother and me. This was to help us get better grades so we could attend the high school of our choice, called Kololo Senior Secondary School which was a five-minute walk from home. He had the biggest everlasting effect on me both in sports and studies plus in the other the extra-curricular activities that I took part in. Music played an important role in my life. Cliff Richard movies from England and Elvis Presley movies from Hollywood started coming to town and hair styles, dresses, shoes changed. Most of the children in the nieghbourhood were Goans who migrated from a Goa, which was once a Portuguese colony in India. Mostly catholic Christians and every house I visited had a piano.

During one of the outings with a school, at a park, underneath a mango tree, I let it all out by singing one of Elvis's fast numbers, "Bosa Nova

Baby" and trying to impersonate his moves. It was a hit and even the teachers couldn't believe the shy little kid had suddenly gone wild, entertaining the little group. I learn't something that day, I could bring smiles to peoples face. I was ready for high school.

Most my school holidays would be spent with my maternal grandfather, Ishvarlal Mehta with whom I have fondest memories. He had finally left the tea estate in Lugazi and moved to Masaka and with partnership with three good friends Tulsidas Karia, Amratlal Jobanputra, and Ramji Karia started a printing shop, acquiring latest print machines from Germany. This was in the basement but the first ground floor had a stationary supplies store. Soon they were supplying stationaries and printing

Left to Right (Sitting)

Punnag Hazarika, Naresh Patel, Manoj Patel, Head Master - Mr. Sheriff, Class teacher-Mr. Surinder Singh,Jayshree,Satya, Urvashi Shah.

Left to Right (Standing)

Dutta, Arvind Talwar, Tejinder Singh, Prakash Pradhan, Kaur, Mahesh Shah, Deepak, Subhash Patel, Veena Patel, Akber, Prakash Joshi, Suresh, Himatbala.

Left to Right (Back Row)

Joginder Singh, Jasbir, Ramesh, Alam, -------, Hemant, Charles.

(1957)

material to all the government offices schools and businesses. As he soon retired and my uncle (Shirish Mehta) took over the business, he had more time for us.

He had a separate room for himself. There were two beds on either side of the room. I slept on the left bed and would him on the right when I visited him. He would get up at 5:00 am, have a quick bath and would sit in lotus position in front of the temple start is prayers, reciting "gayatri mantra" gently moving the 108 Rudraksha beads with his fingers one by one. He would then recite the vedic shlokas from the holy hindu book of "Geeta'. After this he would do "prayanam", breathing exercises and finally he would conduct a 'havan" a religious ceremony performed that involves worship through the use of a sacred fire. He would take some wooden sticks, place it in copper pot and then add "ghee" (clarified butter) and using that as fuel he would light the fire. Reciting "mantras" he would add herbs, rice etc into the fire. Through the mantras, fire is asked to take the prayers and consumed offerings to the intended Divinity. Often, I would ask my aunt about the sudden presence of the red "kankoo" (powder) and perfumed rice arround the temple floor. The aunt replied, "This kind of miracles often happen with "Bapuji", arround the "mandir" but he says nothing about them to anyone ". I was amazed with his ever-present aura of peace, no matter how much mischief we kids were up to, he always calmly sat us down and told us stories, "Here, sit down, I am going to tell you about this mischievous "Brahmin kid". There was always a lesson to learn from the stories, whether it was a about a kid, stupid monkey, clever crow, a cunning fox or a very brave lion. I would get up and take my bath, get ready and accompany him to the shop. It was two miles away, walking in the cool morning breeze with the early morning sunshine and with hardly any traffic or noise but the chirping of the birds. He would open the shop door at seven while my uncle would come in his Opel at 9:00 am.

One day he asked my aunt for some clothes, I helped loading at the back of the truck, then we went to the shop to get some books, stationaries and said to me, "son, let's go for a ride". After say half an hours ride, on the outskirts of Masaka we pulled into a small village. For the first time I was face to face with Africans who had Leprosy. Seeing disfigured faces and limbs was shocking and remember feeling very sad and to this date never forgoton those faces. To-date I have also been asking people from Uganda, the same question if they had ever visited a Leprosy village. **I still have to find one person who did. It has been such proud moment for me that at such young age my grandpa made me realize the true meaning of giving and sharing without expecting anything in return.** There were lot of Africans who worked in the "printing press" coming from small villages, surrounding Masaka, on their bicycles, they were all looked after well by the company, paid well and all appreciated having their own kitchen and shower.

He oftened took us to see movies but the highlight of all the entertainment was the American show called "Holiday on ice". It was something new. Skating on ice with such flexibillity and ease with little

comic acts was a must for every kid to see. We took off from Masaka eighty miles from Kampala, with grandpa in a Peujeot truck. Grandpa started speeding towards Kampala to make it in time. We both brothers were at the rear, covered by the tarpolin canopy peering through the rear window and seeing the speedometer needle hitting 70-80. It was raining hard but grandpa did not slow down on a sharp corner, the truck left the road and overturned. We all took a summersolt . All were safe and pleased to get a ride in another passing by car which was also headed to the show which was being held at the newly built Lugogo stadium. The truck was left in the ditch to be pulled out later. The show was fantastic but we felt for grandpa as he was grounded and not allowed to drive again, instead he was given a driver.

I did well in the final exams at Demonstration Primary School and was admitted to Kololo Senior Secondary School but already there were challenges in the beginning of the first year.

School Days in Uganda- High School

The school had about two thousand students and about ninety qualified teachers just like the rest I would have to take eight subjects and at the end of four years I would be expected to pass all. Mathematics, English, Geography, Art,

Physics, Chemistry, Biology and Gujarati/French. As I spoke my mother tongue (gujarati) well and as I had an option, I decided to take French instead but I lasted only one class and the shock was tremendous, of trying to learn a totally different sounding language in class. A year later when Jyoti started High school, he had no problem taking French. I had already picked up three Indian Languages, gujarati, hindi and punjabi through friends. English was the national language. I picked up Swahili through an African servant, "Francis", a part-time servant who had left village to look for work in the city. After I came back from school, we were often seen sitting on the dining table, me teaching him English or trying to learn chords together on a Spanish guitar which he seem to do better than me, My Swahili improved as I also practiced it with my African class–mates like Patrick Juko, a Bugandan, too. During recess I was often seen sitting amongst the poor African students while most of the Indian students went out to get snacks. There was a definite lack of intermingling between the African students and Indians but while in class there was lot of harmony especially if the teacher was the target. There was lot of interaction when it came to plays, debates, competitions and discussions in general but more when it came to sports like soccer. African students preferred soccer or foot-ball as it was called in Africa, Indian students preferred cricket and field hockey.

Mr. Rawal was the headmaster and not only did students shake in his presence but so did the teachers. I remember once while in class of Mr. Kavi (His dad was apparently a very well-known poet in India) who taught us gujarati and was amongst the gentlest of the souls and never hit anybody, Mr. Rawal happen to be making his routine rounds, (a tall man, would walk a little bent, his hands folded behind, twitching up and down as he marched around the school) saw students making a lot of noise and said, " What are you waiting for, Kaviraj, straighten those rowdy bunch". Mr. Kavi for the first time in his life went into action, picked the nearest of the students and started slapping them around as the class, shocked went "pin –drop silent". As it was the sixties and pop bands in England had tremendous influence on the youths, some students decided to go against the school policy of having only short hair. They were confronted by Mr. Rawal taken to the office where their hair was cut on the spot. There were times when boys who wore extra short "shorts", literally got hold of them by Mr. Rawal and asked, "are you wearing an underwear or shorts, go home and change". The shy Indian girls would smile and just leave the scene. Having white uniform was a must, you were stopped at the gate by the "askari", Mr. Rawal's African watchman who told him of all the news in detail of all the latest happenings in the school ground. Smoking was an absolute no no.

CITY OF KAMPALA, CAPITAL OF UGANDA

SUBARB OF KOLOLO FROM "WIRELESS" HILL AND KOLOLO SENIOR SECONDARY SCHOOL

Due to Mr. Rawal's strict rules, Kololo did well academically. During his rounds of the school if he found a class without a teacher, he would invite the whole class to his office and offer very interesting reading material to students and speak to them about their problems. He had travelled abroad and contracted teachers from countries like USA and Britain. I remember being taught by a Scottish, English, "Walish", Irish, and American teacher. Most of the teachers were from India, a few from Pakistan and an African teacher called Mr. Obyello who taught Drafting. I remember him well, he was very good but had the habit of throwing a blackboard duster at the student not behaving.

Studying under various teachers was fun and all had their unique way of getting across. Mr. B K Amin used to teach us history. On the way to India his ship was hit by a torpedo from a German battle ship, he had a close call, he jumped into the Indian Ocean but was eventually rescued. Due to this tragic experience he got irritated and his big bulging eyes told it all, when the corrugated tin roof shook and rattled due to the howling wind and rain but I still remember part of the British/India history he taught and on the reasons why the British were looking for India, this was his explanation:

"Dear students, do you know why Britishers came to India, they were looking for this cute Indian "chick" called Miss CD"? He would then right "Miss CD" on the board. Now he had our attention, especially the boys, the girls were curious, too but who the hell was this Miss Cd, there would be a pause and he would turn back to the board and then clarify:

M -for Moslem

I - for Indigo

S - for Spices

S - for Silk

C - for Cotton

D - for Diamond

The whole class would burst out laughing but the message was received.

The assistant head master was Mr. Figueredo who taught chemistry had a clever way of remembering the first two rows of the periodic table by remembering two sentences, the first letter of every word would denote a metal.

<u>L</u>ike <u>b</u>ees <u>b</u>utterfly <u>c</u>arry <u>n</u>ector <u>o</u>f <u>f</u>lowers

L-Lithium, B-Berillium, B-Boron, C- Calcium, N-Nitrogen, O-Oxygen, F-Fluoride

<u>N</u>ature <u>m</u>agnificiently <u>a</u>llows <u>s</u>imple <u>p</u>lants <u>s</u>ome <u>c</u>hlorophyl.

N-Sodium, M-Magnesium, A-Aluminium, S-Silicon, P-Phosphorus, S-Sulphur, C-chlorine

The only time there was a total distraction in studies amongst boys and an indirect ways on to the girls is when an English teacher wearing a mini-skirt entered the class. Due to the strict dress code which applied to the school, both meant for the teachers and students it was quite a surprise how the young lady slipped by wearing the mini-skirt. There was usual disruption in the class and it was only due to the presence of Mr. Rawal that some studies did in the end continue. Mostly the Indian lady teachers wore Saris and students were very respectful of them except for this short, slightly plum teacher called Mrs

Patel who walked with a little "spring" and was strict and the boys would whistle the tune from John Wayen's movie called "Hatari shot in the Serengeti National Park and the name of the tune was, "Baby elephant walk".

Block system was introduced by an English teacher called Mr. Ray Gregory. Students were put it to groups and each group were given assignments, produce a newspaper, work on a play/drama to be performed in front of the rest of the group, prepare presentation on research carried out on various subjects and so forth. The system nurtured a team spirit, interaction between students, both boys and girls, too, leadership skills, confidence building and lastly reason to be competitive and have fun too. Unfortunately it lasted only few years as the system lacked the class-room advantage of learning English language grammar skills.

Then there was the American math teacher, Mr. Birel, six foot tall, slightly short sighted who spoke to you bringing his face so close that the noses touched, who introduced basketball to the school which actually became quite popular. Besides having a soccer field, a cricket ground, two tennis courts, Kololo was fortunate in having a basketball court.

I was sixteen when one of my Goan friends called Herman de Souza took me to William Fernandez's home. A family of musicians, they had a band and were looking for a vocalist. The band consisted of William, only fourteen years old (who played piano, part-time for Toronto Hilton Hotel, the last time I talked to him on phone in 2005), he could read music and played both piano and clarinet, Anthony Dantus with whom I played cricket at school played base electric guitar, Peter Fernandez ,a neighbour and a good friend played the rhythm guitar, Mike de Souza played Violin, Lala Patni, a class-mate played the drums and finally Herman looked after the P.A. System. They checked me out and I was part of the band and with vigorous practices we started performing, firstly in Community Halls (Kampala and Entebbe Goan Institutes) then in night clubs (La Quinta and Suzzana) where I got paid and gave my first earning to my mother, 100 shillings and kept the rest to buy myself a personal mike. At seventeen I appeared with my band (The Savannah Swingers) on Uganda T.V. for the first time and in the same year The Savannah Swingers performed at "Pop '67 competition held at the famous Kampala National Theatre. The bands participating came from Kenya, Tanzania plus local Ugandan Bands amongst my favourite was "The Drifters", mostly made up of Goan brothers who played extremely well.

The band started with a slow number, "Sloop John B", the audience was quiet and attentive. The rest of the band had white jackets with a tie, I was in black wearing dark sun glasses, though it was all show the glasses were actually meant to hide my nervous eyes. But this was a competition and I had to get the judges on my side. For the next number I did a "180-degree turn", with my hips swaying and my feet with black Italian shoes loosely swinging, I grabbed the mike stand at an angle and with best impersonation that I could do of Elvis whispered, "Mmmm Kiss Me Quick", the band took off and all I could see through my glasses was the first few rows of seats with girls going crazy, screaming, some pulling their hair, and some were on their feet. I could hear the audience going wild but my kids to this day have a hard time even imagining this, their dad whom they have only seen performing Indian semiclassical music, sitting down, legs folded on the stage, has been a total vegetarian all his life, never drank alcohol, could have ever rocked on stage-unbelievable.

Next day at school, I was famous but my brother who looked like me, but combed his hair much like Elvis did, more handsome started getting complements from girls about the show, he shared this with me, many moons later saying, "Bro, I wasn't going to tell them I wasn't "Elvis", I flirted and said that I would sing one just for you, babe". "So, what happened then", I asked. "Next day when I met her again and tried to chat her-up, she totally ignored me, I was shocked, somehow she had found out the truth," my brother laughed and so did I. Jyoti loved tennis and also during holidays made some money in working at a bookshop.

Sometimes I would be coming home around 3-4 am in the morning after singing late all night but my dad never questioned me. The only time he did say something was when he came to our bedroom once and saw the wall covered with the posters of the rock n' roll bands, The Beatles, Rolling stones, Yard Byrds, Hermann and the Hermits, Monkees, Animals, Dave Clark Five, The Kinks, etc and said, "maybe you should have just a select few".

While I was busy with the band, my dad kept up with Indian music, giving private shows and also appearing on Uganda T.V. I would once in a while accompany him on tabla (drums), playing simple beats called "Kherva" or "dadra". He encourage me to play tabla and take classes but my heart was in singing. My uncle, father's middle brother, Rupshanker Joshi was also a fine musician so it seems it was all in our genes. My maternal grandfather who didn't sing nor play any instrument had the most knowledge about Indian music, he was also a devout listener. During school days we studied hard and there were often very late nights. I used to often study with a very good friend of mine, Raju C Patel, for short we used to call him RC, keeping each other awake, taking breaks, drinking coffee. He did not live too far so it was easy for us to go home and retrieve anything in case we forgot. He often talked about the Kololo School Mountain club which he had been involved with for the past few years. He was a year older than me, one class up. We planned a hitch-hiking trip the very next school holidays.

As soon as we came close to our holidays, we started preparing for it and tried to put as much in the rucksack as possible and as much as we could carry. The main destination would be to climb Mount Elgon, located North East of Uganda on the border of Uganda/Kenya. The towns on the way, going East, would include Lugazi, Jinja, Kakira, Tororo and then going North to Mbale (climb Mt. Elgon which lies on the outskirts) return to Mbale and head further north to Soroti and then to the town called Lira. At Soroti we climbed the "Soroti Rock".

The 1145 sq km Mount Elgon National Park includes shell of an extinct volcanoes although hot springs that we saw still bubbles on the caldera floor. It has five major peaks and the two we climbed, the highest one called Wagagai, is 4.321 m above sea level, making it the fourth highest mountain in East Africa and Jackson Peak which is 4, 119 m. We started our climb early in the morning and crossed numerous lovely streams.

Mount Elgon is an important water catchment for the Nzoia River in the East which flows to Lake Victoria. Climate is moderate dry and slopes consists of a rich variety of vegetation ranging from montane forest (a cloud forest also called fog forest, characterized by a persistent, frequent or seasonal low-level cloud cover exhibiting an abundance of mosses) and at higher open level moorland shredded with giant lobelia and groundsel plants. Even though it was safe and steady climb, at times, we had to be careful crossing narrow paths or hurriedly assembled timber wooden log bridges over deep crevices. The one-day climb took us to the base camp called "Saza hut", it was getting colder and darker, we had time to have a quick meal and slipped into our sleeping bags. The African guide made a small fire and barbequed a mongoose which he had captured somehow. He then wrapped himself in a thick blanket and went to sleep. While we had covered ourselves from nose to toe to beat the cold, he had walked all the way up bare footed, neatly balancing this blanket, wrapped around a four feet long stick, on his head. Next day we were on our way to visit the bubbling hot springs but had to spend some time around the most beautiful sight, a picture perfect, completely round crater lake called Lake Tan. The hot water springs were looked more like a flowing stream filled with rounded rocks. I enjoyed jumping from one rock to the other dipping finger into the hot water and checking the temperature consistency, not a bad place to be when the ambient temperature was on the cold side. On our way back the guide took to one of the numerous caves on Mount Elgon. We did not dare venture in too deep due to lack of flash light but heard stories about the caves at lower level of the mountain being frequently visited by night visitors such as elephants and buffaloes come to lick the natural salt found on the cave walls. Kitum cave, with overhanging crystalline walls enters 200 m into the side of side of Mt. Elgon

Kololo Senior Secondary School Mountain Club—1969

Buvuma Island-Lake Victoria

Mount Muhavura South-West Uganda

Michael Sequeria / Prakash Joshi

Accent to Mt. Muhavura

Bus Station, Maaji Jaaza, (Kabale to Kisoro)-Sunday 7th, December, 1969

Next day we tackled Jackson Peak. Though the face was steep, the formation of the rocks on slopes was such that it looked like natural steps carved out of the side of the mountain, disorientated rocks but you could easily jump from one rock to the other and keep on moving up. I started climbing up and moved up reasonably fast to the top. As RC and the guide reached the top, I saw both of them smiling, I asked the reason why. The guide who had kept quiet most of time said to RC in Swahili, referring to me, "He is not human but a monkey". I took that as a complement and smiled. This was not common at all for him to witness, usually the Indian city mountaineers who visited were in pathetic shape, in fact a large group who came from Jinja made it hardly to Saza Camp, saw the hot springs and the cave and turned back, never attempting the peaks. But this monkey climb would be nothing compared to the actual "drilling "that RC would endure after he left for London, England for further studies. Not having enough money for studies, he joined RAF, Royal Air Force and survived conflicts in Ireland, in Folkland, in Cyprus, and in Desert Storm. Keeping up with him during the hike from Kampala was a tough task as I had to

"Laughingly tell him the true meaning of hitch-hiking meant asking for rides on the way". He would have probably walked all the way from Kampala to the highest peak on Mount Elgon if I had not managed to stop a few trucks/cars on the way.

Climbing the highest peak, 'Wagagai' on the third day, took more time and the spectacular view from the top was breath taking. The guide gave up on us for taking too long, decided to take a quick nap, while we just kept on looking and admiring the long Rift Valley on the East side of the mountain, towards the Kenyan side of the border.

The very next year I joined the Mountain club and RC was in charge of the camping trip the club took to Buvuma Island which lay in the middle of Lake Victoria. There were about fifteen of us, we first took a bus from Kampala to Port Bell then on to a boat to Buvuma Island. We docked at a pier and suddenly from nowhere appeared an Indian gentleman, a sikh. We had expected a few people, Africans living on this isolated island but not any Indians. He had an African wife and traded in lumber. We located an open area surrounded by the thick forest and we were ordered to pitch three tents, one for the instructors, one big tent for us, members and a small tent for the food. We fetched lumber from the forest nearby and made up a dining table with a bench which consisted of one horizontal log placed on two "Y" shaped legs buried in the ground. After supper, we had hot chocolate and sat around the camp fire as it started getting dark. The glittering moon and its reflection on the surface of Lake Victoria made one of the members go to the tent and dig out his portable radio. As we all wondered what he was up to, suddenly some exciting news blared out of the little radio. Commander Neil Armstrong and his partner Buzz Aldrin had safely landed on the lunar surface. The date was July 20th 1969. Apollo II had been launched from Florida on July 16, 1969. We celebrated the event and discussed the project late into the night.

The next day started with early morning exercises, squad drill and a run. Daily routine duties like making meals and cleaning up dishes were posted and so after carrying out assigned tasks and after having breakfast, vigorous training would take place. But before making breakfast there was an incident which would take place that took everybody by surprise. While making the hot chocolate the previous night somebody had left the can containing sugar open. As we peered into the food tent, horrible sight greeted us, all the items were covered with vicious red ants, there was a moving carpet of them, suddenly realizing that every inch of the floor on which we had slept, too was underneath crawling with this insect, we had no choice but respect nature and creatures and tread carefully for rest of our stay on the island. The training started with commando crawl. In another case a rope tied on a tree branch about twenty feet high had to be climbed, grab on to a pulley on the top which would take you down another sloped rope and you would crash in a net down below. Having done lot of pull-ups on the basketball steel frame at school, I remember the astonished look on my friends faces when I volunteered to climb up the rope and did so like a monkey, without much effort to hook up the pulley on the top. The day ended with an obstacle course race, between groups, jumping over bushes, crawling under logs, walking on logs, and swinging from ropes. Once at night while sleeping we were woken up by the instructors, told to get ready as we were going for a walk in the jungle. It was pitch dark and there was one instructor with the flash light leading the way and we followed in a single file. I was the last one in the line and could hardly see anything in the front just barely hear the footsteps of the person in front of me. It was fun though; I did occasionally look back to see if there was some animal tracking me.

Few days before our return three of us went for swim in the lake. The first one dived came up on to the surface and so did the second one. As I dived, I dived further down, something tore into my right leg/knee, my first instincts said, "crocodile", I turned and swam as fast as I could to the pier. The cut on besides my right knee was deep, I was pulled up, and as I was getting a bandage, others worked on making a stretcher, I was then thrown on a logging truck belonging to the "sikh" gentleman and transported me to a visiting doctor who used just warm water to clean my wound and stitched my knee up without any anaesthetics. I was very grateful to the doc, my friends and the "sikh" gentleman and mostly that it wasn't a crocodile, probably a very sharp object. My buddies do laugh about the incident, reminding me of the fear on my face and how fast I swam back, comparing it with a "cartoon movie". I was moved from the tent to the log cabin belonging to our "sikh" friend whose African wife nursed me well but I had to cut my visit to the island and return home quickly to have my leg checked properly. My knee heeled quickly but damage to the nerves is noticeable as when I touch the injured area it feels I'm touching somewhere else. I was following in the footsteps of my dad who had injuries and broken bones throughout his body.

During my four years at high school, I would travel extensively in Uganda. My family with few friends would visit Murchison Falls National Park (Murchison Falls- where the world's longest River, Nile explodes violently through a narrow cleft in the Rift Valley escarpment to plunge into a frothing pool 43Meters below. We took a boat ride on River Nile and at close hand looked at the crocodiles and hippopotamus. On another occasion I was invited by a Patel friend to visit his uncle at Fort Portal on the South West side of Uganda near the Congo border close to the famous Rwenzori Mountains often called "Mountains of the moon". Higher than Alps the ice capped mountain range has the third highest peak in Africa, The Margherita Peak at 5109 m. We were three friends, a "Patel", a "Shah" and myself a "Brahmin" who took a train from Kampala to Masaka and then on to Fort Portal. The uncle was kind enough to let us borrow his car and so we were lucky to see the Rwenzori mountains and visit Kasese and the famous "Kilembe Copper Mines". A day trip to the famous Queen Elizabeth Park had hardly any tourists at the time we visited. For the first time I read the road sign which you had no choice but to obey. It read, "Elephants have right of way". I remember waiting in a car for 45 minutes until a group of elephants crossed by". There had been instances when a driver had honked, irritating the elephant and the car was toppled. This was such a beautifully preserved national park and you could see various animals at close counters. The Park is known to consist of about 100 types of mammals and over 600 species of birds but we were only able to see, lots of elephants, tons of hippos, buffaloes, antelopes, monkeys-chimpanzees, giant wart hogs and water bucks. There was plenty of bird life but could only name a certain common ones like shoe bills, horn bill storks (about four feet tall), hawks, crested cranes (National Ugandan bird), king fisher and cuckoos.

I remember visiting a lodge on top of a hill looking over the Park, run by an English family. Tea and cake/biscuits were delicious and the scenery just beautiful more so with the setting sun with elephants marching towards the water hole and hippos bouncing up and down in the water.

There seem to be a hidden agenda for my mountaineering and camping adventures including the vigorous training, though I was enjoying every minute of it. The Senior Mountain club members (President- Sachdev Singh Seyan and Chief Instructor- Raju C Patel) were leaving school and as I was going to be there for the next two years doing "A" levels, I was approached and during a walk on Kira Road convinced me to take over the job as Chief Instructor of the Kololo mountain Club which also included selecting two boys and two girls from about 100 participants to go for the Outward-bound Course and climb Mount Kilimanjaro.

While dad was at the Post office, dad would buy old cars, clean them up, polish them, get us to clean the engine with kerosene and even get us to use black shoe polish to shine the tyres and then sale them at a profit. His love for cars got him a job at Motor Mart as a cashier. As a cashier he suddenly realized that the sales personnel made much more money than him. He approached the English manager and asked him if he could sale cars. He laughed and wrote him off. My dad persisted and asked to be tried for at least a week. The manager gave in. On the very first day he sold three cars to his old loyal friend, Surayakant Patel who had done well in business in Nairobi, Kenya and now opened a pharmaceutical shop called "Universal Pharmacy" on Kampala Road. His fourth car was sold to Ramesh Patel, another school friend whose father, Haribhai Patel had opened up a law firm called Patel and Patel Advocates and the Partners were Ramesh Patel, his younger brother, Arvind Patel and cousin Chandrakant Patel. His two main hobbies, playing cricket and music got him in touch with lot of friends and soon for the first month of working at Motor Mart he broke all sales records. He was finally making money. It was time to finally build our dream house on Mulago Hill, from its balcony we could see the beautiful Baha'i Tempel. The dream house would be occupied by the American Embassy personnel and the rent would help pay for the two brothers studies in England but would never be occupied by the Joshi Family.

Mother was always kept busy; dad would be bringing customers for lunch without much notice. There would be people coming from small towns who would be very knew to the city, he would bring them home, and mom would feed them. We had a dog called "Rex", a black dishound absolutely a "riot", then there would be Jyoti's and my friends visiting plus guests. My mother had her hands full and the only time she did really get angry was when she came down stairs one day and found her Living room in shambles. She liked to keep the small apartment absolutely clean and orderly, even the dog was trained not to enter the kitchen. Sometimes while playing with us and chasing us we would run into the kitchen, he would brake suddenly and skid with the kitchen floor mat, realizing he had entered "No trespassing "zone, take tumble, with his rear legs in the air and his mouth kissing the floor, he would shoot out.

While standing outside my home, one day I saw an African student cyclist come down the Kennethdale Drive, he was coming down pretty fast and lost control while taking the sharp corner. He was bruised badly and bleeding. I carried the bike home, helped him into the house and was struggling to get some bandages to cover his bleeding leg and arm. The living room was in a mess and "Rex" was barking. Mom came down the stairs and saw the door wide open with a damaged cycle sitting in the doorway, and saw the back side of the cyclist in shabby clothes sitting on her clean sofa and the room which looked as if it had been hit by a tornado. She "flipped out", shouting and complaining about the status of her living room but soon cooled down when I told her the whole incident. The traffic in our home has not improved but has worsened over the years and we can all blame my grandfather who always said, "Treat guests like god".

But this was my final year (1968) at high school and I would have to work hard to pass "O" Levels with reasonable grades to be admitted to two years of "A" levels which one had to complete and pass in order to attend university. The final exam paper for "o" levels came from England, I managed to pass acquiring Grade A.

I had spent most of my time with a friend I had made a year ago, Arvind Patel. We would study together and soon became very close. He was the class clown and used to stammer. Every time he spoke the whole class laughed. I remember him starting a fire in a chemistry lab. He got slapped in Mr. Rawal's office because he suddenly let out a laugh and when asked about it later, he said to me, "I couldn't help it, I saw Rawal's foot underneath the desk, it was very funny, nice pants and shoes but the sock had curled up, oh! It was so funny". It was out of pity that I spent time with him seeing him made fun off nearly every day. I soon came to know from his mother that she had to visit India and had to live himalone with an aunt at a young age. It was this temporary loss of mother's presence and fear that had caused this stammering. The mother added, "But "Beta" (son), ever since he has been with you, his stammering seems to have improved". His dad, J B Patel was a Physics/Maths/Chemistry teacher at Old Kampala Secondary School. Arvind asked me to help him in Biology and in return he and his dad helped me in Physics. He beat me in all subjects, making a career in electrical engineering, assembling half a million-dollar test equipment for the engines of planes. He resides in Michigan.

The next two years of "A" levels at Kololo would be most challenging for me both in terms of deciding whether to go into "Arts" and take up Law or a related field as it was in Geography, I had the highest marks in "O" levels. But I was concerned about job opportunities so turned to "Science" and go into Medicine, Pharmacy or Engineering which I found hard but took a chance and so I had to take up Biology, Physics, and Chemistry.

Kololo "A" Levels and Depart for England

No sooner the year started, I was overloaded with studies and homework. I decided to give up music which took up lot of my time and the late nights over the week-ends were too hard to handle. I left field hockey and for cricket somehow, I had lost interest, soon after my idle and hero, my dad stopped playing, too, after he had a severe injury while playing and fell running, between the wickets. Sachin Ramesh Tandulkar, my current idle, was not born yet so I took it pretty hard when my dad had to leave his favourite sport. He had 13 stitches on his left elbow. He had scored 97 runs for his club (Wonderers Cricket Club -Started by Suryakant Patel) when he fell. They were playing on Makerere University ground against the University team. Makerere University was home to many post – independence African leaders, including former Ugandan President Milton Obote and late Tanzanian President Julious Nyerere whose army finally over threw Idi Amin's brutal regime in !979 while rest of the world slept. Current Kenyan President Mwai Kibaki are also Makerere Alumni. John Noronha, my Kololo neighbor and one of the key persons to help organize the Kololo School Reunion in Toronto in 2001 is a Makerere alumni, plus other neighborhood Kololo school friends and Makerere graduates present included Herman Desouza, Peter Fernandes, and Anwer Omar.

The reason I remember dad's injury well as it was also the day Uganda gained Independence from Britain, October 9th 1962, Milton Obote from the Northern tribe of Acholi was sworn in as the first Prime Minister of Uganda.

But there was one task I had to accomplish and a promise to full fill before settling down with my studies. Help organize and lead a mountaineering hike up Mount Muhavura which involved twenty– seven students which included four girls. Also known as Mount Muhabura, the mountain is an extinct volcano located on the South west corner of Uganda, it's part of the Virunga chain that spans Rwanda, Uganda and Zaire. A steep cone shaped 13500 feet (4127 m) high mountain which is rocky and carpeted by grasses and small shrubs.

 The preparations included, getting permission from Mr. Rawal who threatened to close the Mountain Club down if the girls were at all mistreated or if there was any "hanky panky" on the trip as he put it. This meant taking extra care and visiting parents of each girl and giving them a detailed idea of the upcoming trip, people involved with the responsibilities, list of previous trips taken, and first –aider Michael Sequeira) on hand. Prabikiraat Singh Seyan (President of the Mountain Club) and myself were able to make sure the parents had a reasonable comfort level and I couldn't blame them either as there were no adults accompanying the students. The participants went through proper physical training on weekly basis and were briefed on the conditions of the mountain, one day steep climb, water being the most valuable commodity as there were no streams or any water available during the climb.

Soon we were ready for the trip. The bus ride from Kampala to Kabale on the base of the Virunga ranges would take us one day but as we approached Kabale the winding roads on mountain slopes, lakes, and rivers reminded me of the beautiful scenic ride in Kashmir by bus which I had taken when I was very young. At Kabale we found a school to put us up for the night. I remember some boys wanting to go to town for dinner and were given permission to do so as long as they would come back in time. It would have been o.k. if the boys had apologized but they decided to put their watches back to fool me that they were actually in time. An example had to be set for not obeying simple instructions especially when we were heading for a pretty challenging the very next day. I instructed them to follow me in a single file, marching out of the school in the cold dark night, lining up in front of the thick hedge. They had their backs towards it while I was facing it. I gave the order, "attention" and the next part of the squad drill which they were not prepared for, I said, "About turn, now go through the hedge, I'll see you on the other side". They did and remembered that for the rest of the expedition".

Next day we were at the base of Mount Muhavura, it looked like Mount Fuji of Japan. Three tents were pitched, one for the members, one for the four girls and one for us. African guide was hired and the ascent took place at 7:00 am the next morning. Two boys gave up after a few hours as it was very steep for them and they were asked to return to the base camp. It was a very clear day and the magnificent view became even better as we climbed higher. As we neared the peak there were quite a few boys who literally screamed due to severe cramps, even the salt tablets with enough water didn't help the climbers. I tried massaging their legs and that seem to help. As some of us early climbers reached the peak and waited for the rest what welcomed us was the most beautiful crater lake that we had seen. It is said that the peak on a clear day provides travellers with the most spectacular view from the top in the world. The incredible panoramic view includes, Virunga volcanos and peaks, Queen Edward in the Queen Elizabeth National Park, and peaks of Rwenzori. But there was no time for even a photo shoot. As soon as the last batch came up, around 4:00pm which was already getting late as "a day trip "should have meant that at this particular time we should have been back or close to the base camp. The last batch had hardly time to look around as it started hailing. We ran for nearby bushes for shelter hoping that the hailing for soon stop. I waited a few minutes and gave the order to descent. Two things worried me, it would soon be dark and getting frost-bite. There were certain parts of the mountain were so treacherous with narrow paths that a little lost of balance and foot hold and one would disappear for good down the mountain. I lead the way with the guide and asked Prab to stay at the rear with the flash light to keep eye on the group in front of him. We had a few extra flash lights for people in the middle but soon the batteries died. As we climbed further down the hailing and then rain stopped, it wasn't as cold. My main concern was for loosing somebody down the mountain in the dark. In order to keep track of every member I invented a system by which everybody shouted their number. I shouted "one", then the guy behind me would shout "two" my ears would be focused entirely until I would hear Prab with last of the number, "27". Then we would repeat the numbers again. At certain narrow parts of the mountain, I would ask everyone two sit down and come down on their butts. Half way down one of

member became very sick and had fever. I took over his rucksack so now I had two, one in front and one at the back. Three quarters of the way down, the flash light flickered on to some huts and asked the guide if there was any way we could rest here. He asked the owners and decided to spend the night here. There were a few huts and we made sure everyone managed to get some sleeping room. Prab and I found some corner and were soon snoring. It wasn't until I got up in the morning that I realised that the warmth that I had felt on my back was because I was sleeping on cow dung and actually slept in a cow hut but no one complained and soon we were at the base camp. Thank god we were all safe.

On our way back we stopped at the beautiful Lake Bunyonyi, nine miles from Kabale where we had a picnic, celebrating our terrific ordeal. Thinking back, I realized the expedition was slightly ill prepared but also thought of another trip taken by another group to Mount Elgon a few years before ours, Jyoti accompanied this group, with a teacher present where a tent caught on fire due to a propane stove, a girls hair caught on fire and couple of boys had second degree burns. I was only 19 when I took this trip and learned a lot. I am glad when the time came to say "Good Bye" to this beautiful country unlike the majority of the people who only saw the cities and national parks that I had the opportunity to see nearly every corner of it and made it possible for some to do so, too, including living with the locals.

The first year (1969) of "A" levels seem to be going just right, the class consisted of lot of the students I had known during high school, the "O" level days which had about six classes each year with about 40 students in each class, A, B, C, D, E, and F. The students were placed according to their grades. The one with best grades were in class "A". I was in "C". But all had an equal chance in appearing for the final "O" level exam and then decide what they wanted to do. While some took on jobs, some went overseas to England/States for further studies, some went to India. Some like us who had reasonably good grades, stayed behind and took "A" levels. So it was much a smaller class. I missed my "C" class friends as they had moved on. I remember one of those friends who went to India and later was one of the only friends who made it to Vancouver BC, where I had finally settled and we were once again united. On his 50th Birthday party he sited an incidence which I had completely forgotten. Vraj Sudra said, "I owe my life, my wife and job to Prakash for helping me in the "O" levels exam. It is important for me to mention about this as this was the only time I felt I had cheated in anyway or at any time, in school, but not for my sake but to help a desperate friend. To most of us "Art" as a subject didn't seem to be very important for our careers. This was also true during the exam as even the teacher supervisors were much relaxed, seen going in and out of the class-room Vraj was sitting next to me during the exam consisted of having a painting a portrait of vase with a bouquet of flowers. I started the exam and was soon done painting it but when I looked on my right, Vraj had panic written all over his face. I took his half-done painting and gave him mine. I took time in finishing his painting as it needed some work. After Doing my share I returned his painting and gabbed mine. We both passed the art exam but he had achieved more marks than me. He then applied for Architecture at a

Indian University where he met his wife and then migrated to Canada and found job in his field.

I was nominated as the school prefect and joined the Safety committee where the only tragic incidence I was involved in was when an African student tried to commit suicide by hanging himself in the washroom. It was due to financial hardships. He was saved and the school staff helped him out. As a good listener and often caring, sometimes I got into awkward situations where once I was asked by a friend to talk to his girlfriend and help patch up with her. In doing so, the girl seem to be falling in love with me. This was shocking for me as I believed in true loyalty in friendship and love was sacred to me.

Soon I would fall in love with a Brahmin girl with beautiful green eyes in my class. This was a difficult situation as I had to "live by example" being a school prefect and that too with Mr Rawal being the headmaster seemed at that time a bit challenging. Things did not improve as soon I was elected Head Prefect of the school and studies became the top priority for me as I felt it was getting harder for me. This for me would in the end turn out to be both sad and tragic part of my life.

The campaign for head prefect ship in 1970 came as a total surprise to me as I had not much to do with it. Few students whom I had accompanied up Mt. Muhavura had already started the campaign without asking me. They started going from one class to the other campaigning for me. I was both touched and humbled by this gesture. There were two African candidates and three Indians. The only thing for me to do was to make a speech during the daily morning assembly which started with morning prayer and a student reading key news items from the local newspaper "Uganda, Argus" and though I don't remember exactly what I said but I do remember speaking from my "heart" while others read it out loud, not saying that they did not speak from their heart but this has been my weakness all along in public speaking that even though I might have something written down, I still revert to ignoring it and thus forgetting some items as I start try to pass the message across.

The election results for the Head Prefect were going to be out soon but there was a delay, Mr. Rawal called me into his office and said, "It is a landslide victory for you but I would request you to consider something, as Uganda is a newly independent country, it will be good for Kololo to have an African Head Prefect".

I was taken by surprise and wasn't prepared for this as I had not even thought about the outcome very seriously as not being elected would be a plus as I would be able to concentrate more on my studies. My reply to Mr. Rawal was swift and to the point, "I agree with you, sir but if I have a say, I would like to give all my votes to the second African candidate as he and his campaigners were absolutely clean but the others played dirty, tearing out my posters, etc". He said, "Thank You", and I left wondering which one of the African candidates will he pick?

The next day he came to the morning assembly and announced, "Prakash has the highest votes and therefore is the Head Prefect for the year 1970. My supporters cheered and clapped.

Due to a high student enrolment, there were two shifts, the morning shift which I was in and Jyoti was in the afternoon shift. We saw less and less of each other. He passed "o" levels and requested dad to send him to London, England for further studies. He agreed and soon we were at the Entebbe Airport, with mummy crying. We both brothers were unseparable and this parting was very hard for me, too as all this time we had shared one room and shared inner most secrets Dad called him on the side and said, "There's condition why I am sending you of to London, studies only, no partying, no drinking, no eating meat especially beef and no fooling around with white women". We brothers would later laugh about these conditions as he broke all of those and one condition he broke even before he reached London. As the plane took off and the meals were served, Jyoti started eating. He noticed the passenger next to him, not eating the served meal.

"Kaka, (uncle) why are you not eating, food is delicious", said Jyoti

"Because, I'm a vegetarian, "said Kaka

"I am a vegetarian, too", said Jyoti

"YOU WERE!", replied the Kaka.

He later broke all the conditions my dad had laid down and married an English girl and is very happy but for me life would take various turns and falls and both of us would laugh at fate.

Waiting for the 1970 exam results was driving me crazy, all I required were passes in three subjects to get into a university, either at Makerere or in a university in England. I failed to even get one pass. We were soon visiting Mr. Rawal for advice. My dad spoke first and asked what's the best recourse, what he said would stay in my heart for the rest of my life, it was a fantastic moral boost.

Mr Rawal said, "For a son like this, you should give your life away, send him to London, there's still time before the universities open, he can repeat the exams there which he can't do here". As I had sometime before the results came and making the trip I decided to work. I decided to go to Masaka and through my uncle, Shirish Mehta I got a job at Public Hill Primary school as a teacher. Teaching Grades 5 to 7, History, maths, geography, science and also substituted for an Arts teacher. There were mostly Indian and African teachers but it was always difficult to find one to participate in P.E. I took up the challenge and was often seen playing soccer on the fields with students. I always had gifts for the kids and by the time I said good-bye, there were lot of tears shed amongst the students. Uncle/aunt had two kids by now, a daughter Meera and son Milan. Ramila Metha, my aunty looked after me well. With the help of my uncle I was also able to get a driver's license.

But my most precious time was spent with my grandfather, discussing about the rich Indian Heritage and the myth of Aryan invasion, the homeopathic medication that he relied on, the Indian freedom fighters like Gandhiji and Vallabbhai Patel or Monks like Swami Vivekananda who first came to states to attend "Parliament of Religions ", in Chicago in 1893. He represented Hinduism and was the last person to address the delegates. Handsome, dignified-looking, and only 30 years of age. He was dressed in flowing, orange-colored robes, with turban to match. "Sisters and brothers of America!............" he began. Instantly thousands leaped to their feet, with deafening applause of admiration and delight!

The oddly-dressed man had greeted every one "a sister or a bother "as very appropriate to the theme "love of fellow human beings". To this man, all of were members of his own Universal family. It would take a full two minutes for the tumult of applause to subside.

While listening to some Indian "raagas', grandpa would be seen with tears rolling down his cheeks, in appreciation. This scene would often appear in front of me during later years of my life when during rehearsals, whilst playing harmonium and singing, I would "hit" certain notes. I didn't realize then that this would be my last days spending with only living grandparent that I had ever seen or known and the very next year he would peacefully pass away, without any sickness.

My parents came to leave me at the air-port but they wouldn't be alone for too long as my brother would return for a holiday soon.

My dad and mum-crying wished me well and I jumped in the plane thinking of whatever happened to the pretty green eyed Brahamin girl.

Performing at KSSS annual "Open House" event in 1967 with loud drums echoeing in the still dark night, right accross the distant Kololo Hills. Prakash Joshi (author) and Ashok Babber, never realized that they would years later end up in the country of "First Nations People", Canada.

Munich, Germany. Olympic tower /stadium. Left Bottom: on route from Munich to Frankfurt, my Nigerian friend in red, Okee Eken.

New Brighton Park
Hail, Rain or Shine

She kept her promise,
She would meet me, Hail, Rain or Shine
At the New Brighton Beach Park,
As she got off her bike, completely drenched,
She smiled and said, "No pain no gain, hope you're fine" The circular rock bench alongside the rocky shore, Underneath the umbrella I had waited, completely dry,
Except for the thrashing of the waves,
And the gentle whistling of the breeze
There was no other sound, Even the seagulls didn't cry. And again, the words were hard to come by.
Was that rain on her cheeks or tears of joy,
Once again, she left me, amazed,
How could someone love so much,
Without even giving it a try.

Life in London and The Asian Exodus

My first experience on arrival in London at Heathrow airport was not very positive. I asked for a taxi and a Mercedez Benze pulled over. All I needed was an ordinary taxi but somehow being new and not knowing what was available, I jumped in, greeting the driver and giving him the address. As soon as the taxi was on the road the white English driver said to me, "I do not understand you Indians, you drink the cows milk but don't eat it. "I acknowledged his concern but no words were spoken rest of the way.

My brother lived in East Finchley with a school friend from Kololo. The friend had his sister and cousin living with him. My brother and I shared a bedroom but we hardly saw each other until the week-ends. I would get up around five o'clock and distribute two bags of newspapers. I would then quickly get ready and take the train to Modern Tutorial College where I would get help to prepare for my exams. This is where I met Okee Ekena, a Nigerian and we became very good friends. Amongst the teachers was a young man, Bhan Sinha, who taught Chemistry. He was born in Fiji, studied in Australia, moved to England. I would meet up with him in Vancouver where he finally settled at a function in Vancouver and have remained good friends.

After the "A" Level exams, during summer holidays, I got an opportunity to go to Germany and Belgium with Okee who with a few friends in conjunction with a charitable organization decided to collected funds for the orphans of Nigeria/Biafra war. This meant standing on the street all day, with placards hanging from our necks and shaking tin donation cans. The trip took us from London to Dover, at the East cost of England by train then on to ferry to Ostend in Belgium from where we traveled by car passing through Munich in the South of Germany to the Northern City of Hamburg. It was in Munich, the city preparing for the 1972 Oympic games that I was attacked by some Nigerians. It started by one of them saying, "You don't even look African, what the hell are you doing all this for?" I proclaimed," I'm African, I am a proud Ugandan, a citizen.....". Before I could finish the sentence, he was on me, trying to tear away the placard. It was in a matter of seconds when German police in disguise, suddenly appeared from nowhere, while two of them took him away the other one asked me if I was o.k. and asked me for my documents for charity work. Everything was in order and he left me. I was shaken, but what had taken me by surprise was that just because I was Indian, I couldn't be an African. This truth would haunt me especially when the very next year Idi Amin's dream would result in an exodus of nearly 60, 000 Asians from Uganda. The Nigerian who had attacked me had looked upon me as supporting the break-away region of Biafra province from Nigeria. I was again convinced by the rest of the Okee's friends and by the German family affiliated with the charitable group whom I had stayed with that the entire cause was to help the orphans. I carried on the work until I reached Hamburg.

With the hectic schedule I couldn't see much of Munich but I was able to visit the beautiful churches, the Olympic tower and from the top, I could see the Olympic stadium being constructed. While In Hamburg, I visited the huge harbour which is the heart of the city and the bus tour also passed through a bombed church. As Hamburg was destroyed in the second world war and has since been reconstructed, there are not too many historical monuments left in the city. I did visit the magnificent Alter Elbe tunnel constructed in 1911, a 426 meter long, underneath river Elbe. On the whole I enjoyed the three weeks in Germany, travelling through the Black Forest, seeing the lovely absolutely clean villages with lovely gardens. During 70's I found that as the diet there consisted mainly of meat, I was very happy to find at least one Chinese restaurant in every town I visited, ready to serve me vegetarian chop suey. I parted with my friends, in Hamburg, thanking them for the opportunity to do some volunteering work, taking a long train ride from Hamburg to Ostend then on to a ferry to England.

Jyoti, an article-clerk working with a Jewish accounting firm, called Goldberg and Associates then, seemed to be most impressed when I got home after three weeks, with all the traveling/lodging plus all the day to day living expenses paid for, with 50 pounds sterling in my pocket which seemed a lot during those days.

I passed the "A" level exams and enrolled at North East London Polytechnic taking "Industrial Chemistry". There was a definite divide between the English who seemed to be more reserved and the foreign students. I made friends with Greek, Italian Indian, and African-mainly Nigerian students. The English professors though were very helpful, especially the European professors.

With hectic study schedule and long travel time (one and half hour each way) didn't leave much time for anything else, though I did join "Judo" class. I found out later that it was a bad mistake as I could attend only a few classes. I was reminded by a friend that there would be an exam in order to go to the next higher level to achieve the belt. I attended the test, unprepared. The instructor gave me a theoretical exam, asking me to demonstrate various throws and judo moves which had all Japanese names. I failed miserably, not even getting one question right. So, I was definitely out of the class not even a slim chance of attending the practical exam. You needed to pass in both to go to the next level. I pestered the instructor to let me at least try one bout with someone. I must thank the English instructor of giving me a chance or was it he had enough of this little brown guy, only 5" 4" tall and wanted me out of his hair. He picked one English student, much taller and heavily built than me to have session with me. As required, we both grabbed with our right hand the opponents left sleeve and grabbed opponents' right collar with the left hand. We went around in a circle a couple of times and then I turned suddenly throwing him over my shoulder and pinning him down on the floor. The instructor was surprised. He then asked me to take on another English gentleman who too was bigger than me and once again I did the same but this time it took much greater effort. He called me aside and awarded me the belt. Unfortunately, the late-night training and reaching home late and sometimes having to cook or share with household duties with others didn't live much time for anything else. Judo had to go.

It was October 10th, 1971, Jyoti and his friends living with us had taken off to Uganda for a holiday. I was all alone and really never got used to the life in London. T.V. was a good company but going anywhere cost money. I was always concerned about the financial burden I was causing my parents even though dad kept on saying, "Don't worry son, I am doing quite well now." All people talked about was the weather. Neighbours hardly spoke with each other. I found myself either running for the bus or the "tube" (underground train). I was saying to myself, "As soon as I graduate, I'll be back in Uganda". Suddenly the doorbell rang and somebody said, "Happy Birthday". Mountaineering friends again, RC Patel, Harish Sodha, Nilesh Kangadia and rest of the gang took me out for dinner and a movie. What a pleasant surprise!

It was in Uganda, in the sixties, when T.V. first came to town that I saw for the first time some Black artists performing, Jazz artists like Louise

Armstrong and Nat King Cole, Calypso singer Harry Belafonte, soul queen Aretha Franklin, rythm & blues singers Ray Charles, B B King (visited Uganda in '60's), Rock and Roll king Chuck Berry, reggae artist Bob Marley just to name a few and not forgetting the groups like "The Temptations" and finally the ever popular Gospel singers like Mahalia Jackson. I would compare it to the Congolese music played localy and appreciate the common sense of beat. My Indian sikh friend, Gurpeet Singh who I met at the college and had spent all his life in London further increased my interest and everlasting love for this music. He shared with me early historical recordings of slave songs with me, sadly with no name mentioned of the artist. The recordings also included my favourites Jimmi Hendrix and Marvin Gaye. Full credit goes to Gurpreet for taking me along with him to see James Brown.... what a show!

There was another interest and hobby which we had in common, reading. We often spend spare time at the world famous book store in London called Foyles. One of the first book I picked was "Mans rise to civilization", by Peter Farb which consisted of a detailed description of the various tribes in North America and one was as different from the other as the English is to Chinese. How Eskimos were different from Cherokees or to Apaches or to the Amazon tribes. How some lived in shacks whilst others in two storey log cabins. They had often been lumped as one, "Red Indians". This was a great introduction to the country; Canada I would move to next-know the natives first. Reading would be a good pass-time for me as the tube train rides were long and there was hardly any kind of entertainment on the way, unlike train rides in India.

But there was one incidence that I would always remember. I was standing at the tube station and decided to wait for the next one as the one standing at the station was completely full. The West Indian platform guard shouted, "mind the doors". An English gentleman with a black suit, walking stick and a bowler cap tried to climb up into the train even though one could see there was absolutely no room. The doors closed and caught the Englishman's rear and the doors retracted. It happened a couple of times but the gentleman refused to step down. The guard was about thirty feet down the platform. He sprinted towards the stuck gentleman and kicked the gentleman in his rear and as he did that, the doors closed and the gentleman in his typical English accent screamed, "thank You". I burst out laughing and the West Indian smiled, it was all in a day's work, to keep the train moving and keeping the system running smoothly.

I passed the first year at the Polytech and during the summer holidays I got a job as a stockman in liquor store. It was wealthy area; I did see Rod Stewart pay a visit once. I must have just worked a few weeks when my Dad called and said, "How are you doing, son?". I told him about the job. "He said, "Hell with the job, come down here and I've planned a holiday to Mombasa". I was in a plane the very next week. I met up with a few friends who had stayed behind and also visited Masaka to see my uncle and aunt. I had hardly been there a week when Idi Amin announced that he had a dream from God.... giving Asians holding British Passports three months to get out". There was some confusion as to whether he meant Asians citizens, too. But my father didn't want to take any chances, I was out within nine days, back to London. My mother followed soon after, having a British passport, she had no problem entering Britain. My father refused to leave as finally he was doing well in Kampala and thought things would settle down and he would have no problem as he was a Ugandan citizen but he was forced to leave, a year later.

I had my work cut out for me as soon as I got back, my uncle who had some money saved up asked me to find a house for him in London. His brother in-laws who were much senior to me and well settled were very busy. Jyoti was working and trying to prepare for charter accountancy exams. It was left up to me to balance my studies and look for a house. I saw this as an opportunity to help my uncle and learn something. I saw numerous houses and the Real Estate sales representative was getting pretty tired of me and my questions. Finally I found one, a semi-detached house which would give some privacy plus it had a very big lot, with a park and school nearby. I asked my uncle's best friend who had been living in London for several years, had a good job plus a house, for some advice and his reply was, "This is between you and your uncle," he replied. I was only 21 years of age and had been in London for about a year and my uncle had entrusted me with a task. I bought the house for him for 13, 000 pounds. It is worth about 350, 000 now. It is amazing what you can accomplish when you have a sincere desire to help, no matter how inexperienced you are. In years to come lot of people would seek my advice, even though I would have no knowledge of the subject and even admit to my ignorance and it could be on various issues, careers, job interviews, business dealings, community services, leadership skills, confidence building, sports, drama, relationships, marriage, divorce or simply broken promises, the urge to help was so strong that the answers simply worked themselves out. I tried to use every negative one as a learning experience which I had plenty to share from but turn that into a positive one. This is the power of caring and helping that my elders had reinforced on me.

My uncle, aunt and the kids lived in a refugee camp in London and were looked after well, after fleeing Uganda but soon all of us were together living in the newly purchased house in South Harrow. Mummy started having a part-time job, Jyoti continued with accountancy putting in long hours, my studies were interrupted and I found a job with an engineering firm, Messrs Sandberg working as a materials technician on West Hendon Highway project. My uncle started working at Dabenhams, a department store. Everyone chipped in. But horror stories from Uganda kept on filtering through. We were all very worried about my dad being there by himself. As he was amongst the very few Asians who were staying behind. Most of his time was spent at work or transporting people from Kampala to Entebbe which had numerous army road blocks, harassing fleeing travelers. Each person, according to Idi Amin's order could carry only two suitcases and that too were often checked several times at this road blocks so that the army could help themselves to any precious items like jewellery, watches, etc. Not too many volunteers could be found during that time to escort refugees to the airport.

It was after one of these trips, after living his friend, Ramesh Patel at the airport and returning to the famous Speke hotel that he was confronted. (He had left home and booked himself into Speke hotel which seemed more safer). He decided to park his brand new "demo" car at a more convenient location. As he pulled out a black Mercedez came around the corner and flashed the head lightes telling him to pull-over. As he stopped two army officials came out of their car and ordered, " Muhindi !("Indian" in Swahili), get out of the car, you don't know how to drive". They started beating him up, he fell and covered his face as they started kicking him, the army boots taking a heavy toll on him. They pulled him up again thrust a gun his stomach. He thought that was it, they were going to kill him, thinking quickly he said, "Why are you beating me, take my brand-new car, the papers are in the hotel room, I'm salesman and I'll transfer the car to your name". This is what saved him. He took them to his room, transferred the car and gave them the car keys.

Next day he was standing in line at the Canadian Embassy. One of the staff saw his condition, severely bruised and took him inside and asked the reason for the abuse. Within 15 minutes he was given Canadian visa. Next day he was on the plane to Kenya first, where some close relations had him checked out by a doctor and then he took a flight to London, England. As three of the family members were already in England, we thought we would have no problem in having him join us. We went to see him at the camp where he was detained and we did have some legal assistance. The British immigration thoroughly interrogated him and learnt that even though he had Canadian visa he had intentions of joining his family in London. They put him in the first available plane going to Vancouver, British Columbia.

As for us two brothers, we decided to carry on working and supporting our mother until dad was ready to sponsor her. We kept in touch with dad to see how he was doing. We learnt Vancouver was one of the most beautiful cities in the world with beautiful snowcapped mountains, stayed evergreen throughout the winters, and also had mild winters too. Had more parks than any other city. Life was easy and you could at least have an outdoor activity once you got home from work. It sounded more and more like Kampala or was it more like the east African coastal town of Mombasa with old light houses-how about sandy beaches? Education system was different, you didn't have to wait one year and pass an exam. The four-month semester meant you got your credit for the particular course if you passed. After passing a number of required courses and having received the required number of credits, you were awarded the Diploma or degree.

It took my dad a year to settle down and then decided to buy a house. He called me and I was ready to move. My brother and I would part once again with a loving hug. On Christmas day, December 25th, 1973 I touched down first at Montreal and was rushed to the immigration office where the officer found all my sponsorship and landed immigrant papers were in order but I was travelling with an expired Ugandan passport. A little lost time, explaining about my current refugee status I soon departed for Vancouver.

This was the first time I had seen so much snow and there wasn't much to see from the plane as everything was covered with white blanket of snow but scenery changed as we approached the Vancouver airport. Just as I had imagined. The pilot flew over the Pacific Ocean and turned around to land with the Fraser River on your right and the snowcapped Grouse Mountain on your left. It was green all over with scattered lakes. The forested peninsula must be the world-famous Stanley Park. "Thank You Prime Minister Trudeau," I was finally home.

Time to say good-bye to 52 Kenneth Dale Drive, Kololo, Kampala, Uganda in flats which we had lived in for nearly ten years before having to leave suddenly for England. (summer 1972)

Canada-Family Reunification

My father never forgave the British authorities for separating him once again from his family but it was a blessing in disguise, in the end. They secretly and forcibly put him on the plane the very next day as we came to meet him again to get him out of the camp. He was being escorted to the plane as we said goodbyes with both of our parents in tears. This was extremely a very sad day for all of us, finally being united once again and then to see a badly physically and mentally bruised man being torn away from his family and taken far away on to the west cost of Canada.

He landed in Vancouver, BC in winter. He was given a winter jacket and refused any financial assistance but asked for a job. His first job was selling insurance, North of British Columbia. Going door to door in severe winter conditions, with lot of snow. He broke all company records for the three months he was there but soon he had a telephone interview with a manager representing Brown Brothers Ford. A car dealership in Vancouver. There were not too many Indo Canadians working as car salesman then, as a matter of fact not in any sales department. There was some hesitancy in hiring him so dad asked him to try him out. There was some hidden discrimination but the manager in general found him working very hard even coming to work on his days off which was acceptable for the company as long as one had scheduled a prior meeting with the client. There was an incident where a finance manager was extremely rude to an Indian client and swore at dad. Dad punched him. In the next sales meeting, the general manager gave him 500 dollars and advised him to take up boxing lessons. He showed tremendous patience with Indian and Chinese customers who usually came with big families to a buy a cars and negotiated a tight bargain. They were tough customers and plenty of times he would show them his commission slip as to how little a profit he was making off them. While some salesmen made a lot of profit on each car and then took it easy for the rest of the month, he sold more cars and kept his profits reasonable. This was long term plan as eventually he would have more return customers and more referrals.

He topped the sales and furthermore he was the top salesman continuosly for seventeen years for Western Canada selling Ford cars. He soon sponsored my mother and was happy finally to have some home cooked meals.

As soon as I landed in Vancouver, I fell in love with the city and the people. I found Canadians to be friendly, honest, helpful but somewhat ignorant of the rest of the world. As one of them put it, "when we heard about Ugandan Refugees, we were expecting people to come down the plane with pots and pans on their heads". Majority of the Indo Canadians who had migrated here were found to be working on farms or saw mills and were mostly from a province called Punjab, mostly Sikhs. Though there were quite a few who had acquired proper education in India, their education and qualifications were not recognized by the institutes here. This was the same with other immigrants.

who came from various countries, except for the ones who migrated from western countries. They would end up working manual jobs. I would later take up this meaningful cause and go as far as bringing their concerns to The Conference Board of Canada, "The Think tank" for the Federal Government in Ottawa. I would also be interviewed by Globe and Mail newspaper from Toronto and Institutes like Association of Professionals Engineers and Geoscientists of British Columbia who had thirty thousand members, to expose this major flaw in our system where proper talent and education was wasted.

I thought I would have it easy as I had come from England and had worked with a reputed firm. No such luck. I couldn't find work in my field so I took up the very first job which came my way to support my dad, working with my dad as a lot man in a car dealership. I only lasted three weeks when the general manager after coming from lunch with his buddies poked fun at me and asked me to wash the car again for the sake of it, one bad look at him and I was summoned to the office. I knew what was coming so I banged the fifty odd car keys on his desk and I was fired on the spot. My next job was selling "china" cookware and "pots and pans, all weighing about sixty pounds, door to door. I didn't do too bad but it was entirely on commission. Each unit sold for five hundred dollars. Soon I was working as a carpenter making kitchen cabinets, this lasted about a year and the owner was quite impressed and offered me partnership but my heart was set to go back to college, I was just working to get some funds to put me through college. I enrolled at British Columbia Institute of Technology (BCIT, taking the Chemical and Metallurgical course) in summer of 1974. I was able to get some credits for having done courses in England. I had some free time so the councillor advised me to take up Bussiness Management Courses at night, surprisingly I got "A's", I was definitely not as good in science, compared to "Arts". During the summer of "75 I worked as a technician with an engineering company called R.M. Hardy and associates. I completed the whole summer and as I was about to say good-bye and continue my full-time studies, Harry Watson by immediate supervisor asked me whether I would like to continue working on week-ends, part-time. "Yes! I will do that for you Harry, as long as you hire me full-time when I finish B.C.I.T. He smiled.

For the second year I took "Pollution Treatment option" at B.C.I.T. As a young man I was determined to get rid of all the Pollution in the world. It seems I was quite a head of my times, In fact there wasn't even an Environmental Ministry yet in either the Provincial or Federal

Government, then. But this did not stop me from making sure that I put all my efforts in helping to keep our planet clean. I had seen lot of floating gas stations around the Vancouver harbour Marinas at False Creek and wondered what the water would be like around the marinas. Dorris my German term project partner and we jumped into her dinghy sampling water samples and nearly got run over by a huge barge. It was a loud blow horn that woke me up. The water samples were tested by Infra-Red analysis at the B.C.I.T. laboratory and we did find traces of oil. My other project was on research of oil polluting tankers which dumped oil and disappeared. I learnt that every oil source had its unique Vanadium: Nickel ratio and after analyzing the oil and determining the ratio one could track the oil source and thus the tanker. As I graduated from B.C.I.T. I didn't even take time to attend the graduation ceremony, I was too busy applying for jobs, two hundred in all. Soon I had to face the truth of the haunting words of a friend who had written in my B.C.I.T. annual wishing me luck as we parted, "in order to find a job in pollution, we have to pollute the earth first". I found Part-time work and finally gave up and went back to Harry. The economy was slow and there wasn't much work around but plus Hardy technicians belonged to a union. I did have to wait but was soon working full-time.

Meanwhile I had a marriage proposal through my parents referred by our relations in Kenya. I was told of a Brahmin girl born in Kenya but living and working in London. I decided to pay her visit, we had chance to talk and exchange some views, considering this was an arranged marriage and would depend a lot on trust, I asked her if this marriage would entirely be her own wish and if there was any kind pressure involved. She said," no there is no pressure". I said, "if there is someone you do wish to marry, please let me know maybe I can help, I have been known to build relations, not break". She smiled and insisted that there was nobody else in her life and I continued, "Would you like to marry me?" She responded quickly, "Do you want to marry me"? I said, "Yes".

I went back to Vancouver and started making arrangements to sponsor her so I could bring her back with me after our wedding in England.

One day as I came home, I saw some gentlemen had paid a visit to our home and were having a serious discussion with my parents. One of them was from Uganda and he was looking for me as a potential marriage candidate for his sister. My mother politely explained that "I was spoken for", just recently.

On further revelations and through mutual contacts in Uganda I asked him about his sister and what school she had gone to, he said, "Kololo". There was only one girl that I knew in Kololo having the same surname as this gentleman. She was the pretty green-eyed girl".

Career High and Break-Up

One day Harry called me into his office and said "Are you going on holidays?" I said, "Yes". "Have a good one, when you come back, you'll be the Lab. Manager". It was nearly a year since I started working full-time. I told Harry," I've no skills for management and most of the guys are senior to me". Harry responded, "I'm not actually looking for a manager, someone who cares and has time to teach people, you'll do just fine".

Soon after I had started working as a Lab. Manager my name was put forward for a part-time instructor (Teaching at night) by my mentor. There were three candidates but I did well due to my teaching experience in Uganda. Furthermore, who would have known that years later some gentlemen would walk into my office and award me important fairly sized projects and say, "You don't remember me, do you? ". "I'm sorry, no", I confessed. "You taught me concrete", the client said. It would be a pleasant surprise but I did remember, after the class would finish at 9:45 pm I would then help some with simple mathematics, until late at night.

Management has its challenges and rewards. The first challenge I had was to go against a Senior

Management in hiring a sikh gentleman wearing a turban. In the ten offices across western Canada Hardy had no person wearing a turban. There were some tense moments in the office but I persisted and encouraged full communication between the Senior manager and the sikh gentleman. The manager found him to be, polite, hardworking and had good English communication skills.

Hardy was a union shop. The relationship between the union and management were not always happy but workable. I was both in the union and took on management duties. Try to figure that one out? Nobody complained. I had an open-door policy and once somebody got hired they were looked after well, trained well and if the time came for one to move on and up they had a good reference letter. I remember firing only one person during my 20-year spell. The only complain I did get was, from everybody, "Why did I take so long, to fire him". This was the other big challenge I did have was to lay-off guys or to fire somebody. I thought everyone deserved a chance and with time and compassion things would improve for everyone.

A technician who was born in Toronto and moved to British Columbia was hired but couldn't open up a bank account as he had no fixed address. I had to phone the bank manager and vouch for him or did I threaten to close my account if the bank didn't accept his well-earned money? The other time an engineer from Philippines couldn't find a place to stay and I persuaded my parents to rent out their basement to them at a very reasonable rate until they found their own place. All this gestures, looking back helped to strengthen relations and trust.

I remember one time when I hired a Chinese Technician, he was desperate for work and we were short staffed. He didn't speak English very well and was often ridiculed by some co-workers. He kept quiet and carried out his work diligently. Finally, it was time for him to move on with his career. He came into my office to thank me and wanted to do something for me and asked me out for dinner. I told him it was not necessary as he didn't owe me anything and the way I had treated him was no different than I would treat anybody else and further more I wouldn't want him to waste money as he was a student. He persisted and I gave into him, thinking I could always pay or share but I didn't have a heart to say no. During the dinner I asked him about his plans and how he happened to be in Vancouver. I learnt he was very well off and had his own house and furthermore he had received a scholarship to study at Waterloo University. There was a technician who had accompanied us for dinner, he nearly fell off the chair and mentioned the news to the rest of the group at Hardy. There was a lesson to learn for the group, "**Don't under- estimate, anyone**".

At one time the company hired a muslim engineer who had just finished a contract with SAR, joint venture company who had designed built the skytrain. Though he didn't report to me directly he approached me for guidance regarding personal and company/career issues. He asked me about a place where he could pray several times a day without disturbing anybody. This is the first time I had such a request as most of the time people did not talk about their religious beliefs, I felt humbled that even after knowing I was a Hindu he felt comfortable in discussing about this particular matter with me. I suggested his office but the offices had large windows and he didn't like the idea of being seen during the prayers. Finally, I found him a quiet a place, a storage area for our old files. The place was fairly big and most of the time the lights were turned off unless somebody was looking for a file. On one such occasion, the secretary came down to the storage room and suddenly came face to face with this gentleman who had actually not turned on the lights. She had not expected anyone as the lights were turned off. She jumped out of her skin and complained. The matter could have been resolved easily but the secretary tried to make a big issue of it, saying that prayers should be done at home. I was able to calm the situation down by reinforcing to the secretary that one has the right to do whatever a person feels during a break as long it doesn't interfere with anybody else. Furthermore, I asked her if a person can take coffee, read book, do exercise, do yoga than why not prayers. She cooled off. The problem was further solved by having the lights switched on by whoever is visiting the storage area.

During this time, I was also approached by John Leech, president and founding member of what is presently known as the Applied Science Technologists and Technicians of British Columbia, ASTTBC which has about 10,000 members. He encouraged me to be part of the council. I was the only Indian representative on the board and volunteered my services for 15 years. My other volunteer duties included being part of the awards committee, career speaker at BCIT, three-member committee of the appeals board and also act as a l liason with some of the other affiliated groups.

The laboratory was a construction materials testing laboratory which included testing soils, concrete and asphalt. I had the opportunity of working in all three departments. Carrying out routine quality control testing and reporting. The engineers were part of the management and there was a definite barrier between the engineers and technician. Neil McAskill was a a senior technician and would get involved in more interesting work, mainly field work, building innovative testing apparatus to carry out load testing on structural members. As a laboratory Manager I would get request to carry out testing on various construction materials, often carrying out investigative analysis on materials failure. Neil and I became good friends as we started working more and more together. He would often build custom testing equipment, all built and assembled in his home basement from where he ran his own business called "Unifab Testing Equipment". As we got involved in more and more complex testing and troubleshooting, the engineers who were part of the management group started considering technicians as part of their team. Hardy encouraged technicians to be Project Managers. Soon Project Managers had chance to build up their own clientele and run projects. In 1980's Hardy got bought over by another Engineering company, Agra Earth &Environmental Limited which had branches all across Canada and the technicians were not part of the union. There was a definite move by the management to de-unionize. The materials testing and inspection division, headed by Harry Watson and with about twenty union technicians, including myself was closed. The company cited economic reasons and the division not turning a profit. The management retained three long term technicians Neil McAskill, Greg Wilson and myself. The saddest part of this situation was to see Harry, the most loyal, hardworking and honest employee of the company having let go. But who would have known that after about fifteen years I would again be back working for Harry who started from scratch and his company (Metro Group) grew having ten branches and 150 people working for him.

Over the years I considered myself very fortunate to have worked on some very large projects in British Columbia such as the ALRT, (Advanced Light Rail Transit) built and finished just before the world-famous Expo 86 held in Vancouver, British Columbia which put the name of the city on the world map. I also remember taking a canoe underneath the Vancouver pier and having to confront a rat as big as a "dog". I had lived in Africa and had come across all kinds of strange animals but never been so startled by a harbour rat eyeing me for a possible meal. This was in preparation of a load test which was conducted before the great Pan Pacific Hotel was built on it. Alex Fraser Bridge (also known as the Annacis Bridge) was the longest cable-stayed bridge when it opened on September 22, 1996 but since then there have been quite a few built which are much longer. My work involved in the Quality Control testing and inspection of the testing facilities of the precast concrete panels used on the deck. During the feasibility study of the construction of the 7.5 km twin tunnels for the 700 million dollar "Seymour –Capilano Water treatment Filtration Plant", rock was tested for Quality Control purposes. The Plant located at the Lower Seymour Conservation Reserve will treat water from both the Seymour and Capilano sources. The water will be conveyed between Capilano and Seymour through underground through this twin tunnels.

My most interesting assignment was to determine the cause of pvc pipe failure during a hydrostatic water pressure test in Vancouver. The pipe fitting ruptured causing a worker to be thrown in the air, several feet high and the injury caused him to spend three days in the intensive care. The parties involved were City of Vancouver, pipe manufacturer, pipe fittings supplier, contractor and WorkSafe. I was first approached by the city but nothing came out of it. Secondly, I was hired by the fittings company to determine the cause of the rupture as it affected thousands of dollars of replacement cost of this fittings if found that there was a material deficiency. After thorough investigative analysis, studying the type of failure and checking for clues using an electron microscope, it was determined that somebody had slammed a 30 kg steel lid on the brass/pvc fitting but this was not evident as during the rupture all the items, including the worker had blown away.

This kind of detective work and having a questioning mind would help me later to catch my cheating wife and a double-crossing so-called friend who help create proverbs like "you do not eat the hand that feeds you".

Soon after landing in Vancouver in a bitter winter morning, I was standing at a bus stop and a gentleman must have picked up from my questions regarding the bus routes that I was new to the city and as a matter of fact also new to the country. We started talking, that had never happened in England. Not only did he talk with me but he was nice enough to give me advice. "So are you new? "he inquired. I said, "Yes". He added, "Well, then be careful of three W's." He said," weather, work and women". I laughed loudly and heartily with a questioning look, not believing it.

I got married and sponsored my wife to Vancouver. The very first week of her arrival in Vancouver we had a call from a gentleman from England, he was called himself CC. As my x-wife picked up the line from another part of the house, I unknowingly picked up the other line thinking no one has yet picked up the phone. This is what I heard.

My wife, "How is your wife"

CC, "I don't need my wife, I have you". I put the phone down. This was clue #1 but it was too early and probably the guy was just flirting and the incidence was forgotten.

A year later on our first wedding anniversary, I had never been so excited getting a gift for someone, as I had a salary increase plus it had been one year since I had been working full-time. I remember jumping about in the mall, running towards the car and finally driving fast to go home and give her the surprise. It was in our room and excitedly I presented her the gift. She opened the box took out the ring and throwing across the bed said, "The diamond is too small". Clue #2

About two years later I suggested having kids and her reply was "I don't won't to have any kids. Clue #3.

About three years later, during an uprising in Kenya, there was an abuse of the Indians by some Africans. Indian girls were raped. I decided to sponsor her parents and a sister. As the situation improved the parents returned but the sister stayed with us for nearly two years.

My son Ronak was born on April 14, 1979. Birth of a child is such a lovely experience; I personally can't compare it with any other experience that has given me such pleasure.

My second son Milan was born on September 24th, 1981. I was very thankful and appreciated that the wife had a change of heart to have the kids but there was no force on my part. In fact, she seemed happy.

Ten years later into the marriage, one night the wife packed her bags and took the rest of her clothes putting into the garbage bags and loaded the car. The kids were watching T.V. both lying on the carpet and asked, "Where are you going". She said that she was going on holidays and will be back soon, but never to return, a long holiday. The kids were only 7 and 6 years old. Her uncle came from Florida and sat us down, I apologized if I had done anything wrong but for the sack of kids she should come back. Her father came to convince her, all the way from Kenya. He said she should return soon but she did not return. Finally, she went to England to see her aunt who had worked very hard during our marriage. She phoned me to get a place for ourselves, away from the parents. I did, a fully furnished condominium which she even visited but stayed empty for six months. I was getting really worried about the kids. Then the rumors started floating about her, she was seeing a man. I asked her and told her "Everything is forgiven" but she did not admit to anything. She started making lot of overseas trips but not alone. I asked my physician about my concern regarding the kids and the lies which did not end and which I had no way of proving. He suggested a detective, I hired a detective and soon came to know, she was involved with a man whom I had given shelter few years ago, when he was in trouble. "Prakash, my wife has thrown me out of the house on adultery charges and I'm going through a divorce, I'm emotionally too upset to live by myself, I will really appreciate your help". He lived for a few months and I did not except any money from him". I had promised that I wouldn't live a single stone unturned to save the marriage but she had made up her mind. The pathological lies for whatever reasons never ended but the real truth came out when the divorce papers were filed, she demanded enough money to trade for giving me full custody of children. She demanded half the portion of the house which belonged to my parents. She was not successful. My lawyer asked for financial support for the kids, as minimum monthly payments but she had planned this well, taking a part-time job and citing not having enough income to help with kids. As soon as the divorce papers were signed, she went back to her full-time job and living lavishly with a guy. Lets now switch places and see what would have happened if I was in her place and she had the full custody of the kids?. In 1980's it was not common to see men have soul custody of children and raising them by themselves, especially if he was an Indian dad. Men usually for the sake of their egos never mentioned the injustices caused by women to them and during those times I heard of many husbands loosing everything they had earned to support their families and seeing all taken away while the wife lived happily ever after with another man. There was less effort on patching up marriages and the lawyers took full advantage trying to fill their pockets and the judges were more sympathetic to the women. I remained strong throughout the ordeal due to the two innocent boys who had been caught up with "two" adults who could not make up their minds. I remember on one occasion when hearing about this incident a friend came to console me but broke down himself and I infact had to give him moral support. This was a shocking incident in my community. Ronak one day realizing the dad was in deep thoughts came to me and said, "Papa everything will be fine, don't worry". The only worry I did have was the effect on children due to this break-up. I had done enough reading on the adverse effects on children due to broken marriages and homes. During all this time I made sure I looked strong in the presence of Ronak and Milan and never let go off my sense of my precious humor and pulling pranks. Secondly, I had not cheated so my conscious was clear. Lastly, I had always said to others that one does not ask children if they would like to come on to this earth, we bring them so it is our full responsibility to look after them. It is a pity that there are no current laws which deal with this obligation. At least couples should go through some extensive course before getting married on having kids and looking after them and should be liable for abandoning their duties, especially their own kids. There should be more time spent on patching up differences rather than councilors encouraging split. Children should come first rather than the selfish egos and materialist greed for more money, or wanting a different partner. One can understand if the partner is abusive but the children should be given the top priority. What are we teaching our children? Is this the reason why I saw high rises full of seniors living by themselves when I was a salesman going door to door, wanting to talk to me. Some were so lonely that they literally held my arm and took me inside their apartments so they can exchange a few words. This was a shock to me. Are seniors not part of the family, do we need marriages, kids, extended families with seniors being part of it? If this questions are not addressed now, sooner or later we shall pay a price in one form or the other, presently in form of the increase in domestic violence that's taking place.

Top photo: 1975-BCIT project, sampling water for pollution near Burrard Bridge in Vancouver, BC. Neil McAskill with author, Nelson Island. Neil built a log cabin, dam and powerhouse on the island.

Queen Elizabeth Park
Meeting of the hearts

Standing on a little wooden bridge,
Over a narrow water falls,
Down in a valley,
Appeared a beautiful garden,
An evergreen lawn,
Surrounded by lovely wedding flowers,
As the two hearts sang, bridging the two,
Photos snapped, capturing the
treasured smiles.

Mans' Best Friend-Kids and the Dog

My single parenting days were most joyous and I would never trade that for anything else. I had now moved on my own with Ronak and Milan to our old home which was very close to my work, just two minutes away. Life became busy, It meant getting up early, around 5:00 am, getting ready, wake kids up at six-thirty and do a paper route, we would then come home, have breakfast and get them ready, pack their lunch, drop them at the baby-sitter who would drive them to nearby Parkcrest Elementary school at 9:00 am. I was able to leave work anytime if they needed me or had forgotten something or were sick. Arround 3:00 pm was usually coffee break at work so there was enough time to pick up kids from school and drop them at the Kensinton Ice Rink for skating lessons, they were too young to tie the laces so that took some time before I got back to work. If they were not skating, they would taking swimming lessons at Eileen Daily Pool or going back to the baby – sitter. As soon as the lessons finished, I was ready to help them get dressed and take them home. It was then time for supper, time for little T.V. and a little play and finally for some homework. We would then gather around to make our own sandwiches. I would give them a bath and then sit down in front of the temple for prayers which was hard for Ronak who was a very hyper kid and had difficulty in settling down. But he did listen and we would start turning the holy beads saying the mantra,

Om bhur bhu-vah svah

Tat sa-vi-tur va-ren-yam

Bhar-go de-vas-ya dhi-ma-hi

Dhi-yo yo nah pra-cho-da-yat

(Let the earth. the entire world and the heavens be enlightened by the brilliant supreme light of Lord sun and inspire our intellect). Once I heard a little giggle and scuffling sound and opened my one eye to see what was happening, to my surprise Ronak and Milan were racing with each other as to who could turn the beads faster. I nearly fell off my lotus sitting position with laughter.

The day would end with me pulling the telephone plug at 9:00 pm, jumping into the bed with Ronak on my right and Milan on my left and a funny story to be told which I would not be able to complete sometimes as I would be so tired that kids would politely tell me to go to bed as I was messing up the story, the monkey story had suddenly turned into an elephant one.

During summer they were either in summer camps at SFU or with YMCA or on holidays with me or with their grandpa and grandma. Easter holidays were often spent on Nelson Island with the MAkaskils. Nancy, Neil's wife had helped me baby sit my kids when they were very young. The kids thoroughly enjoyed the camping trips and two ferry rides on the way there, stopping at the coastal town of Sechelt for lunch. Neil would pick us in his boat/punt from the mainland at Langsdale and take us to his log cabin on Nelson Island. The kids would enjoy the wilderness, tracking in the forest with Rebecca and Jennifer-MAkaskil daughters, watch the bald eagles and fishing in the boat.

The finest surprise that each of the kids ever had and do remember very clearly even though they were so young was when one evening I took them for a long ride. Ronak kept on asking me," where are we going "? I would keep on saying, "to visit someone". Milan wouldn't believe me. He knew dad was up to something. I parked the car in front of a house in Langley. Knocked on the door and a lady welcomed us in and we sat in the living room. She opened one door and there a silver grey keashound came rushing towards Milan and me sharing a sit and jumped on us. Ronak couldn't resist the suspense anymore delighted he said,"Papa, is this for us?". I said, "yes". Brew was hardly a year old when we got him and was with us for the next 15 years giving us the most precious gift of love and joy. We had a dog house in the back yard but he barked so much that we had to bring the dog into the garage. But that didn't stop the neighbours from complaining of his bark. Soon he was inside the house but the barking did not stop. Finally he came upstairs and slept in my bedroom and if accidently the bedroom was closed he would bang his mouth on the door, swing open the door with a bang, waking everybody with a jump. He would then come on the right side of my bed, circle three times, lie down and with a sigh go to sleep.

We have had four dogs in our family to date, starting with Jimmy I the white German shepherd, Jimmy II the golden spaniel, Rex the black dachshund and finally the silver/ black keeshond. The dog was the best guard dog and companion they had. No matter how upset or tired they were feeling, after coming from school but as soon as they saw the dog, every little pain or frustration seem to disappear.

Any spare time I had would go towards music, playing harmonium, singing and composing songs. I had stopped all sports activities and also stopped giving any performances and all my time was spent around them. It was during this time that I met up with an old Ugandan friend and musician. He had spent every bit of his effort in music. A great "Tabla Nawaz". A versatile and master of percussion instruments. He had accompanied numerous international artists and recently had provided music for the Hollywood movie "City of Joy", shot in (Kolkata) Culcutta. He had arrived in Vancouver with a band, touring Canada but as a strict vegetarian asked me if he could put up with me, instead. This was great. He saw the instruments around the house and felt at home. I would sometimes, after talking about the good old days leave him with his tabla to go to bed and to my surprise he would be sitting in the same position as I had left him the previous night, playing tabla.

The practice session would have lasted the whole night. His dedication towards music and his humility was very inspirational. I had composed six songs and he encouraged me to record them. We rented the whole music system and after practicing the songs several times, we recorded the six songs. I greatly appreciated his input and was proud that I had produced something of my own with such a great artist as so far I had been singing songs produced and sung by others. The kids were simply thrilled to have Sirish Manji around. He resides in London, England.

One summer holiday we three, the two kids and me crossed the Rockies, camped at Jasper and drove on to the biggest mall in Canada which had a huge wave-pool, The Edmonton Mall. The kids had always wanted to visit this big wave pool and the water slide. From there we visited the "Reptile World" south of Calgary where they were both happy to have a python over their shoulder but I was just happy to take their photos rather than make friendship with the python. Then we moved to Drum Heller, the world of Dinosur.

The following year I visited my brother, Jyoti in London and the four cousins, Ronak, Milan, Neesha and Nimisha had a great time seeing each other again as the last time they met was in Vancouver. While Jyoti's wife Suzan looked after the kids, I had some unfinished business to carry out. RC and his wife Divya had a surprise dinner arranged for me.

I would finally meet, after twenty long years, the pretty girl with green

The Grouse Mountain
The "Grind"

The cable car ride during summer,
To the top of Grouse, for every guest was a must,
Vancouver view and the surrounding lakes,
rivers and The Rockies would still not quench their thirst.
X'mas company Party during winter was another treat,
With lot of sparkling snow, skiers and as much
you can eat.
I do remember saying to her,
" I would follow her to the end of the world"
The challenge was that, I would have to do
"The Grouse Grind" first.
A steep climb to the heavens and with an every step,
A curse, what people do for love and lust.

My Wife – Darshana

Professor Zamar was a very humble man. He had come to Vancouver on an exchange program. He lectured at NARSEE MULJI Institute of Management in Mumbai. He had come to lecture at Simon Fraser University. As he was by himself most of the time he liked to visit people over the week-end.

Mrs Zamar did not accompany him for this short visit as she ran a medical clinic in Mumbai.

Professor Zamvar met my parents at the temple and they spoke about me. He wanted to meet me. From the temple on their way home, my parents dropped him at my place. I invited him in and he sat down. We started talking and he asked me about my work. Soon we were talking about some overseas trip that he had taken and some strange incidences that had occurred. I shared some very funny incidences that had occurred to me, too. He laughed so hard and grabbed his stomach and rolled down on the carpet. The kids wondered what was happening and saw this gentleman literally rolling on the ground, "Is uncle o.k.?" "yes", I replied and they disappeared. This wasn't the first time that someone had laughed so hard. I was known to tell stories and describe situations with utmost details and found people laugh so hard that I found them in tears. At parties I would tell a joke or say imitate Peter Sellers and that would crack people up. I remember dad, mom, Jyoti and me going to see Peter Seller's movie "The Party", when we were very young. My dad and I have a fantastic sense of humor and while we both were going absolutely crazy with laughter, mom and Jyoti were wondering, "what's wrong with this guy" and were kind of embaressed, didn't want to have anything to do with us. I enjoy a good laugh and feel my sense of humor has helped me break up lot barriers. Even during shopping total strangers have approached me and said, " Do you know, you have the most contagious laugh?".

I offered him some snacks and drinks to cool him off and the discussions turned to a little serious note. He asked me bluntly, "Do you have any intention of getting married again?" Over the three years that I had been single I had a few proposals, including a girl who had come with a drama group (lead actress) who was brave enough to even propose to me directly. I said, "No, I see my first responsibility, to look after the kids. Prof. Zamvar continued, "I know of this nice Brahmin lady who works as a bursar in my university. She was forced into marriage at 17. The husband was abusive, beating her up and demanding money from her parents all the time. Things turned really ugly after they had a baby girl. He asked her to get rid of the girl, she refused. He tried to kill the baby by poisoning her, but she survived. He then threw her on the railway tracks but a "thobi" (Indian name for a person who makes living by washing clothes). He picked her up and knowing the family brought the baby to Darshana. At the age of 18 years, she fled Dehli by train with a police escort to Mumbai, to her parents. I was dumbfounded. I couldn't believe that such abuses were still going on in certain parts of the world. When the wife was pregnant, I was often asked, "What would you prefer, a boy or a girl?" My answer remained the same, "I don't have a choice, so I'll be happy with whatever I have, I love kids."

Prof. Zamvar continued, "She put herself through university and has B.A. in economics, she also has a diploma in Textile Design and Home Science. Her daughter is 8 years old. She lost her motherrecently and her only sister is in States, married. She has been by herself for past fifteen years, looking after her dad now and daughter."

I told Prof. that I really didn't have any time to even consider marriage. I'm very busy and after what had happened to me, I had actually lost interest in marriage. Prof. Zamvar thanked me for my hospitality and as he didn't have a car I dropped him at home.

Prof. Zamvar did not give up and contacted my parents again. My parents decided to make a trip to Mumbai, India. As retirees they made several trips during the year which included, Europe, East Africa, Dubai, Hawaii, an Alaskan cruise, Mexico, India and of course to England to see Jyoti.

They liked Darshana and the little daughter, Tejaswini. Darshana had to be tricked by her friends to even consider any potential prospect for marriage. She was against re-marring as the few Indian men who did want to marry her wanted her to leave her daughter behind with her parents. She met my parents and heard of my situation. Her reaction was very similar to mine, "How could a mother abandon the children?" There was a common thread between us, "children."

As soon as the parents came back, they were on my case. I refused to consider anything even related to marriage. Finally, my mother said, "Son, you have been working pretty hard and need a holiday". Now that was true, I would not attend any social functions which did not include children which included company Christmas parties. I tried to have some time with friends but did not enjoy a minute without my boys. My parents convinced me to visit India, meet my cousin Rajen in Vadodra and see Darshana and if I liked her and the feelings were mutual then move ahead, slowly. I had accumulated lot of holidays and had to take them. My parents offered to look after them but still as I had not parted from them even for a moment, it was hard for me to leave them.

While Darshana waited for me outside the Mumbai airport, Colonel Krishnakant Vyas, her father went inside to look for me as there was such a delay. While he asked for Prakash, the only passenger that the airline could track was "Pet Cash". While Darshana was looking for a guy in a blue suit, the only blue that I had on was my jeans. So when I passed her without realizing it was her as she had a hairdo completely different from the photo I had seen of hers, she was too busy looking for the blue suit not the face. Welcome to arranged marriage II.

I fell in love with her genuine smile. She was most caring and got most of her strong traditional family values from her grandmother, Gulaben Balkrishna Upadhyay. Her grandma had whip marks on her back from the days of the British rule, during her freedom fighting days alongside Mahatma Gandhi. She spends most of her early life with her, remembering that her grandma only gave her the same present every year on her birthday, dress made of "khadi" (Khadhi shot in prominence in the early twentieth century when the Indian political and spiritual leader Mahatma Gandhi called for the public burning of British mill-made cloth, and urged patriotic Indians to wear only homespun Khadhi).

Darshana and Prakash in Singapore

Darshana, her dad Major Krishnakant Vyas and Prakash

Prakash at the Japanese Garden in Singapore, Darshana and Prakash Joshi in Singapore Airport

*First Prime Minister of India, Jahawarlal Nehru
and Darshana's mother Kusum Vyas*

Swami Tejomayananda- Healthy Living

By Prakash Vinod Joshi

Nutrition and exercise not only improve longevity, but also provide a sense of freshness and vitality as well as enhanced mental function (especially in the elderly).

Spiritual Heritage of India

It was in Jinja, Uganda when I was very young, just in my elementary school, that I had the opportunity to see at first hand the miracles performed by the late His Holiness Sathya Sai Baba (one of the 100 most spiritually influential people in the world). Since then I have eagerly and patiently waited to hear the words of wisdom from the swamis who travel abroad and enlighten us with their spiritual sermons. Swami Satyamitrananda visited both Uganda and Vancouver, British Columbia. Late Swami Chinmayananda visited Vancouver in the '80s, followed by Swami Tejomayananda who is presently the spiritual head of Chinmaya Mission. (Today Swami Chimayananda's legacy remains in the form of the vibrant international organization called the Chinmaya Mission. The mission serves Swami Chinmayananda's vision of reinvigorating India's rich cultural heritage, and making Vedanta accessible to everybody regardless of age, nationality, or religious background.) In 1978, I had spent three weeks alongside Shree Morari Bapu taping his sermon on "Ramayana." His humbleness very much impressed me and he made a special mention about volunteers who worked behind the scenes not expecting any reward but happy to serve a useful cause. Dr. N. Gopalakrishnan is a scientist and an honorary Director of the Indian Institute of Scientific Heritage of India. Hearing him makes you proud of being an Indian. I made a special trip to visit him in his home state of Kerala. After attending his several lectures during his two visits to Vancouver, I found his narration of Vedanga (limbs of the Vedas) which consists of customs and rituals (Acharyas) in Hinduism to be most outstanding and detailed both spiritual and scientific aspects of the customs/rituals and how, though written thousands of years ago, they can still be found useful in these modern times to purify oneself in becoming a better person

AUTHOR AND DR. N. GOPALAKRISHNAN

Darshana's mother was a teacher and her father spent most of the time away from the family, in the Indian army, until he got shot in the right arm which made it difficult for him even to write. Her younger sister called Kashmira was only one and a quarter year younger than her. She couldn't stand the strict discipline of the grandma and therefore spent most of the time with her mother. Darshana loved sports and was a good painter. She even dared to do parachute jumping. She took up classical dancing but her most favourite hobby was listening to music. As soon as I phoned home and relayed the news to my mother that we'd decided to get married, Ronak and Milan heard the news and started jumping on the bed. They were getting a "real" mom and a sister.

Tejaswini loved dogs and studied at a private convent school. She was only ten then. She came back from school one day and seemed very worried. I asked, "Sweetheart, what's wrong?" She replied, "I'm going to be in big trouble with mum when she gets home from work." "Why is that?" I asked. "Because, I've lost my compass box at school," she replied.

"Teju, I need a haircut, can you please take me to a barber shop and then I can also have 'tail malish' (oil massage)." I said. I held the child's hand and we went to see the barber. On our way back, I stopped at a shop and bought her a compass box. She couldn't believe her eyes. When she got home Teju said, "Mummy, can I call him Papa?"

Our wedding was simple and during a photo session outside a temple, Teju inquired about why there were not many people at our wedding. I was quick to reply, "Not only do we have all these people but also a dog, look at that dog behind you." She burst out laughing.

Soon after the wedding we took the train to Vadodra, to see my cousin Rajen Metha and family to introduce Darshana to the closest family I had in India. They welcomed her with open arms and, in fact, liked her too. That was a good start. Somehow the "drama girl" came to know that I was in town. The whole of the drama group came to visit me one by one. Finally, she showed up, wanting to take us both for dinner, and she interviewed Darshana wondering why I had picked her as my wife rather than her. Darshana was amused and also felt sorry as she seemed to have really liked me and seemed hurt, but after knowing the truth, that I had not promised or led her on for any reason, she felt better. (The poor drama girl would die a few years later due to a tragic vehicle accident while sitting as a passenger on the rear seat of a scooter and being run over by a truck. We were both overcome by grief even though we knew her for only a short period, but her kindness and love during this time was overwhelming).

Darshana and I planned our honeymoon in Singapore whereby I would then continue onwards with my trip to Vancouver and she would return to Mumbai and wait for my sponsorship papers and then Teju and she would join me later.

Well, the best of the drama was yet to come. Our visas for Singapore were confirmed but only my ticket with Air India was confirmed, not Darshana's. I was happy that at least I would get back to Vancouver in time to start work, but I saw the real side of Darshana when there was any sign of injustice or bias. In fact, she reminded me of "me." This was her turf, her country, her people and she was going to tackle them her way. She blasted the ticket checker, "If the travel agent issued us visas, confirmed tickets, what do you expect my husband to do, **spend the**

honeymoon by himself? As usual, because of the limited number of passengers, you have decided to take on a smaller plane and have thrown your citizens out, making them wait for the next one." We were soon on the next plane, not Air India but British Airlines and she had that beautiful smile all the way to Singapore and also for the four days we spent there until she had to say goodbye to me as I took the plane alone to Vancouver. She couldn't hold the tears then

Singapore was just beautiful, we were happy to have that deserved break as both of us had been so busy with our lives, pleasing the rest of the world, that we had forgotten that there was life beyond that to be enjoyed and this was the perfect spot. The visit to the Chinese and Japanese Gardens, the cable ride from the mainland to Sentoza Island, and the train ride around the Island, and lying on the white sandy beach were all most satisfying. As I pulled her towards me, giving her a hug, we were thinking of the same thing, "How must the kids be doing, how will we cope bringing the two families together?"

When I reached home there was finally time for celebration. There was joy in the air which I had not felt before. The kids were most happy to see me, and the parents too had had good quality time with their grandchildren. My best friend D. U. Patel was there to greet me. But it had to be an early night as I was working the next day

At work the first phone call I received was from my ex-wife, "Did you get married?" she demanded. "I would like to come back." I couldn't believe my ears; she was living with the guy, she was married. "This must be Canada," I said to myself. I've always been proud of the answer I gave her,

"Darshana is so understanding that being a mother, she would probably understand your feelings about coming back, but what do you expect me to say to this 10-year-old girl who considers me as her 'papa' and I've taken her to be my daughter?"

Brew, The Kishound

A blue bird perched on a tall evergreen kept on calling, endlessly
Then there was this woodpecker on a light post going tap/tap marking it's territory
With squirrels darting from branch to branch, my keshhound,
Brew Circled underneith,
barking away like mad and trying to keep up with them, mercilessly.
The crows as usual cried in harmony,
Demanding food which I would throw later, from the balcony,
And also complaining about Brew who would have the first pick, selfishly.
I had once again got up to an early morning delight.

The Family Grows

On December 30th 1990, Darshana and Teju finally departed from Mumbai to come to Vancouver,

BC but I had planned so she could break the journey in London and meet all the relations. At Heathrow Jyoti waited for them to come out of the airport. Looking at the passenger monitor he couldn't see them. He saw one trolley piled up so high up with the luggage and couldn't see the person behind it, it looked as if the trolley had a mind of its own and was moving by itself. Finally, he saw the two little ladies, Darshana and Teju pushing it. Well, they had both said good-bye to the country of their birth and excited about the new home that they were going to. They packed as much as they could especially for the two boys and for Jyoti's and Sue's daughters, Neesha and Nimisha.

As we all went to pick them up at the Vancouver airport, Milan seeing the amount of luggage mom was carrying said, "It seems mom has brought the whole India with her". It was time for adjustment, soon after Darshana and Teju settled into their new home, Ronak spotted a rabbit in the yard and Milan shouted, grab it. So there was one more family member, Darshana, Ronak, Teju, Milan, myself, Brew the dog and "Grabit" the rabbit. I started building a huge tree house which could take about seven kids so there was an open invitation for the kids to come and play in the back yard and all enjoyed Darshana's delicious snacks. But soon there was going to be another addition to the family.

Darshana started working part-time and met an 80-year-old Punjabi lady at a restaurant where she was working who came to drink some tea. She just kept on asking for hot water and spent nearly the whole day there. It was cold outside and she was trying to keep herself warm. When Darshana asked about her situation. She replied that she had been thrown out of her home by the daughter in-law and that she didn't know what to do. Darshana said, "My husband speaks Punjabi and he'll help you". She brought her home and soon we came to know that her husband was a doctor and very rich but before he died, he had transferred all his assets to the son's name. The son became critically ill and transferred the assets to his wife. The wife took over all of the assets kicking the sick son out of the home and also the mother-in-law. I thought I could easily get the lady into an old folks home but to my shock there was three year waiting period for nearby care homes. She stayed with us for nearly two years. She confessed she had no money to pay rent or for food as she needed all the money to spend on the lawyers to fight the daughter in-law. I said, "I hadn't asked for any, stay as long as you want". We also paid for the funeral costs when the son died.

As cash flow was a bit tight most of the holidays now were simple, mostly camping trips and on one such occasion we made the mistake of taking Brew with us but the kids thoroughly enjoyed the trip. The camping site was known as Porteau Cove hours ride North of Vancouver. It was pouring rain. The small Toyoto Corolla I had, had room for only five of us so the children carried Brew in their laps. He seemed to enjoy this tremendously and the hyper dog that he was, would constantly move and turn around, getting the children all excited as he whipped children around with his tail. As soon as we reached the camp site, I realized I had forgotten the middle pole of the tent. I was teased by the kids regarding me being the camping expert. But I soon fixed that by cutting of a branch from a nearby tree. After dinner we took to our sleeping bags and put Brew in the car. Brew woke up the whole camping site, especially when the Whistler train passed by. He was completely drenched with rain but we had to get him into our tent which had just room for five of us. There were a few complaints but soon everybody was sleeping with the smelly wet dog who had found the perfect company.

Loon Lake in British Columbia—Moral Re-Armament (MRA) camp on Canada Day 1998

On June 30th-July 2nd 1998 a MRA (* Moral Re-Armament) camp was held at Loon Lake Camp on the 1200-acre Macolm Knapp Research Forest, near Mission, British Columbia. The organizers were, Chris /Anne Hartnell, Chris Harvey from Edmonton and Prakash/Darshana Joshi. Darshana and me had taken the kids to this site a year before along with the families of Gujarati Society of BC and had fallen in love with the surroundings. It was a perfect setting withe huge cedars covering steep rocky shores surrounding the cool waters of the Loon Lake.

There were about 30 people at the camp with family backgrounds from Uganda, India, Korea, Fiji, England and kids born in Canada, including a special guest from Nagaland.

"On Canada day the programme started with a opportunity to share what MRA meant in our lives, with the stories of honesty in business, importance of the quiet times and the effects of care and love in changing personal relationships. We then considered what Canada meant to each of us, some being quite recent immigrants. We found we had so much to be grateful for in this country and we thought how we could help Canada.
*

I had been the past committee member and also the chair of the "Friends of the Environment "(FEF), affiliated with TD Canada Bank-Burnaby branch. The main function of the board was to assist environmental groups in providing grants. One such group called North West Wildlife Preservation Society was invited to give a beautiful illustrated presentation on the need to preserve the ecosystem.

As we headed home, Chris Harvey wrote in a MRA newsletter, "after saying goodbye to our new friends, it felt like a very fitting way to celebrate Canada Day, in the natural beauty of forest and lake with the new Canadians building their lives on the west coast."

As the family grew, there was a definite need for a van which came to use when seven of us, grandparents, the parents and the three kids made a 6200 km trip south along the western coast which included, Washington, Portland, California (Disneyland & Hollywood studios), Colorado and Nevada states. Cities included, Seattle, Portland, Las Vegas, Reno, San Francisco, Los Angeles, and Sacramento. Brew stayed behind in a Kennel-the most expensive part of the trip. I pushed Ronak and Teju into being part of the Canadian Air Cadets. They were proud of wearing the uniform but the rigid discipline was kind of hard for them though the air-gliding experience at the Abbotsford airport turned out to be a big thrill for them. Ronak, after working summer at the Canadian Tire decided to go on an European tour with his friend. I had one condition for him in order for me to make any financial contribution towards the trip, he would have to visit the MRA reconciliation center at Caux, Switzerland. His partner, a quite a few years elder to him deserted him not wanting to do the same. He was only seventeen then but he kept up the promise that he mad made to his dad. In doing so he got lost and ended up in Genoa in Italy rather then Geneva in Switzerland. He only spend two days but he wrote this in the MRA local newsletter, *"Caux – a place high up on the mountains where everyone from around the world is treated equal- a place where everyone helps each other and respects each other-1996"*

Papa and mummy were getting old and decided to move closer but the property values where we lived had sky rocketed so the decision was to demolish the old house and build a new one. This was done in style. It was Hollywood come to town. I was approached by a Hollywood company making the series called, "The Millennium". The company was ready to pay us, to blow-up our home. Everybody was excited, especially the kids but Darshana was sad as she had very fine memories in the old house. A fifty feet tower was erected near the house for flood lights. The scene to be shot consisted of a lady driving a truck pulling into the drive-way, parking the truck, carrying her little baby, opening the house door and switching on the light and the house blows up causing part of the roof to fly-off, windows to blow-out, causing the truck to jump in the air and the pyrometric system causing a huge ball of fire. The whole neighborhood was there for the party, the kids had invited all their friends from the school. There were lot of smiles around and I soon realized that all the neighbors had got paid for causing any inconvenience. This was a win-win situation. The police, fire trucks and paramedics were on hand to provide any emergency assistance.

The new house was built in less than a year. I would have a new designation, besides being a fulltime engineer, I would also be the official tourist guide. We would receive as much as six groups of guests in a summer sometime and I would have the opportunity to show-case "Beautiful British Columbia".

Lot of the guests would also include people who were associated with "Iof C", Initiatives of Change, formly called, MRA (Moral RE-Armament- Founded by Frank Buchman in 1938). In 1990 I met Chris Hartnell who introduced me to MRA.

"Initiatives of Change (IofC)is a global organization dedicated to" building trust across the world's divides of culture, nationality, belief, and background. The organization is committed to transforming society, beginning with change in individual lives and relationships.

Initiatives of Change programs are active in many countries. In the United States, **Hope in the cities** promotes honest conversations on race, reconciliation and responsibility. In Switzerland, the **Caux Forum for Human security** brings together people working for peace and human security. In India, Centre for Governance works with development experts, policy makers, social activists and others to strengthen role of citizens in governance. Asia Platteau in Panchgini, India is another international conference centre, created in 1967. In Sierra Leone, **Hope Sierra Leone** is active in reconciling and rebuilding the country ravaged by civil war."

"Initiatives of Change International is a non –governmental organization based in Caux, Switzerland. It is the legaland administrative entity that federates the national bodies of Initiatives of Change in its cooperation with the United Nations. In 2009 Prof. Rajmohan Gandhi (grandson of Mahatma Gandhi), was elected President. "

It was through Chis Hartnell and Jack Freebury of Edmonton, both MRA members that I had first met Rajmohan Gandhi and was inspired to write my first article for the local newspaper in Vancouver, British Columbia. The attached articles are based on some of the people that I was fortunate to meet and write about and their peace initiatives.

Canadian Newsletter

Published by Moral Re-Armament from 251 Bank Street Suite 500, Ottawa, Ontario K2P 1X3

Volume 7 - Number 4 *September/October 1996*

Caux 96 - Healing the past - forging the future

"Caux - a place high in the mountain where everyone from around the world is treated equal - a place where everyone helps each other and respects each other."

Ronak Joshi, 17, from Vancouver.

This brief statement by a young Canadian who was in Caux for only 2 days seems to contain many of the essential elements of this extraordinary Jubilee summer, which 52 of us from Quebec City to Victoria, from the Yukon to Southern Ontario, had the privilege of experiencing. We ranged in age from 7 to 83, with 14 of the participants under the age of 30. There were 6 from the First Nations, from communities both in the east and the west. We covered a large variety of occupations - business people, health care professionals, academics (both teachers and students), homemakers and vigorous seniors! We joined forces with others from the Americas to host a 2-week period of the summer, doing everything from peeling vegetables to leading meetings and discussions.

The warmth of the welcome by the Swiss, the calibre of the speakers and lecturers (many of them well-known world figures), the quality of the plays, musicals and concerts presented almost every evening, the life of community in sharing the daily tasks, the babel of scores of languages and dialects and the incredible job done by the translators - all this and more helped add up to a kaleidoscope of hope for the future.

There are official reports of the conferences in preparation which will be available shortly, giving excerpts from speeches by the Dalai Lama, Cardinal Franz Koenig, Chief Rabbi Jonathan Sachs and others, and a flavour of the messages from leaders such as Bill Clinton, Helmut Kohl and many others. In the following pages we want to give a sample, in our own words, of what the time meant to us as Canadians.

Lise Gagnon and Rosalind Weeks

December 14, 1994 — THE LINK Weekday Edition

Meeting Raj Mohan Gandhi

By PRAKASH JOSHI
The writer is currently working with Agra Earth and Environmental as a Project Manager.

In the year 1963, a young man of 28 years old decided to march 4,000 miles from the South tip of India to North, New Delhi. His vision was to enlist millions of his country men as a revolution of a national character to cure hunger, poverty and promote unity. "The March on Wheels" was started on October 2nd (birth date of Mahatma Gandhi) amongst them were people from all around the world. Amongst these people was a couple, Sarcee Reserve Indians from Calgary who flew to Madras October 16, 1963 to join the march. Another Canadian from Edmonton, Jack Freebury had joined the march. It was with Jack and his wife Mary Jean who had welcomed me to their home that I patiently waited to meet the grandson of Mahatma Gandhi, Raj Mohan Gandhi and his wife Usha.

In early morning winter walks, in Edmonton, I had long chats with Jack Freebury, telling me about his stay in India and the work of Raj Mohan Gandhi. It was also Chris Hartnell my English friend and his wife Anne Hartnell who had made this trip from Vancouver possible for me. Anne Hartnell had donated her air mile points to me for this trip. As Chris and I sat in the plane, lot of questions ran through my mind.

Chris who apparently left a good paying job in England, in the seventies, had decided to work with Raj Mohan Gandhi for his newspaper called "Himmat". Each week Raj Mohan Gandhi wrote an article. The article was a loud and clear voice of reason and justice. The article was often quoted on every continent on papers as different as South Pacific Post, The West African Pilot, The Times and Time Magazine. His comments on leadership made strong impression on use of the European head of government that he had then copied and circulated to his cabinet with a note saying they would all have them read before their next session. Chris spent 3 years with "Himmat," sharing his printing abilities and getting inspired by the views of Raj Mohan Gandhi, working without a salary.

My first visit with Raj Mohan Gandhi who stood, six feet (Mahatma Gandhi was 5'7") was at a reception held at the dairy farm (just outside Edmonton) by the Bocock family. The Bococks had spent several years in India and had invited Raj Mohan Gandhi who was attending a conference.

In Minnesota, U.S.A. the Bocock family have contributed significantly towards the Panchgani Center, several hundred miles from Bombay. In 1967 the first work camp on the new site was set up. From a little shed with no running water the site has been transformed into an accommodation for hundreds of people. It has taken four years of hard volunteer work and stands beautifully as, "Asia Plateau", providing full time work for about 200 people, a training center for men and women, a world conference centre and, "A Beacon of Hope", as Sunday standard called it. In Raj Mohan Gandhi's words, "you give us the land, we'll give you a centre!!"

During the two receptions held for Mr. Gandhi a lot of interesting discussions took place. Raj Mohan Gandhi was only twelve years old when Mahatma Gandhi was assassinated. For the last 6 months he had visited his grandfather daily at the Aga Khan Mansion (prison) and was greatly inspired by him. He talked openly about corruption and poverty in India and how there was a lot of work to be done. The population explosion was under control but would surpass China in few years. The notion of people that politicians are "crooks" had to be changed. He had taken upon this political career to enhance harmony, unity, and corruption and stamping out poverty. India was self-sufficient and the open market system had worked. He was very well versed in international affairs. His recent travels in South Africa, Russia and his peace making trips to troubled Assam are well documented. His recent visit to Pakistan and, an interview on television was unedited. The Muslim world was amazed at a "Hindu" writing a book on the lives of eight great Muslim leaders. His genuine smile, honesty and his comments regarding Indians not being very good listeners were very well taken. His talk on listening to "The Inner Voice" was remarkable. He presently works with Institute of Policy Research in India, residing in New Delhi.

As Chris and I left Edmonton we talked about Raj Mohan Gandhi's planned visit to Calgary. He was visiting the Sarcee Indian people, especially the widow, Rose Crane who had marched along with her late husband, Leonard Crane with Raj Mohan Gandhi in 1963. He was also received with a pipe ceremony at the "Morley Reserve of the Stoney First Nation.

Raj Mohan Gandhi was in Edmonton earlier this month from December 6th to 8th, 1994.

Raj Mohan Gandhi seen here with Prakash Joshi during a recent visit to Edmonton early last week

The historic visit of His Holiness the Dalai Lama

by Prakash V. Joshi
April 18, 2004

Vancouver and India by its Multicultural and Multi-faith nature could be an example for the world. Dalai Lama and Nobel Laureates visit leaves lasting blessing for Vancouver.

Much is written about the historic visit of His Holiness the Dalai Lama. Who was joined Archbishop Desmond Tutu from South Africa and Professor Shirin Ebadi from Iran, the three Peace Prize recipients.

I was privileged to be present at the two public events at Pacific National Exhibition (PNE), University of British Columbia and Anglican Christ Church Cathedral, plus at a media conference at UBC, representing The Link and joining the group of 400 journalists in an effort to capture on tape, film and words some highlights and wisdom expressed. Here are some of my impressions from theses encounters.

The first Public Event was held at PNE on April 18, 2004 to a capacity crowd of 13,000 people. His Holiness Dalai Lama spoke on Spirituality and elaborated on the nature of compassion, on the many ways of cultivating a good heart in order to help others and how to live a fulfilled life while serving, good heart-Full Life. He commenced by recognizing Canada as a multi-racial country. A special mention was made about India where for thousands of years, people of different traditions/faiths (Hindus, Muslims, Jains, Zoroastrians, Jews, Buddhists, Christians, and Sikhs) lived alongside in harmony. In fact, he mentioned Muslims in India were closer to other traditions/faiths than Muslims in Indonesia or Malaysia. Even though he kept on referring himself to be a 'simple Buddhist monk' and eventually launched into a detailed explanation of Buddhist values and analyzing the spiritual and philosophical nature of 'I / Self', he was all the time conscious of the presence of large number of non-Buddhists in the audience and encouraged to keep their own faith and become better. He described the three poisons of the mind, attachment, hatred and dissolution and the importance of deep value for fellow beings and having an ethical mind. 'Moreover let the conscious be your witness'. Mindfulness of the everyday life to finally achieve an eternal transformation.

In the afternoon, at PNE, it was again a complete sold-out event. His Holiness Dalai Lama spoke on 'Universal Responsibility'. His longtime friend, Archbishop Desmond Tutu delivered a fantastic upbeat and a humorous introduction. He spoke of an incident in San Francisco where a young girl, all excited had come running to him and said, "Pleased to meet you President Mandela". He added this kind of a mistake would never happen with His Holiness as he is so well known around the world due to the positive energy and warm heartedness with a bubbling laughter that he imparts. Even though his Holiness had been in exile for 45 years, living now in India and 80,000 Tibetans have followed him, he had still not shown any signs of bitterness towards China and would like to resolve all issues through a meaningful dialogue.

His Holiness spoke on materialism, desire to want more and more at the cost of human exploitation and the environment. There is general agreement amongst all including the learned regarding the decline in family and cultural values. As people become more self-centered, selfish, greedy, children are neglected. It is scientifically proved that persons who are self-indulged, using 'I', 'me' and 'myself' are more prone to get a heart attack. As there is greater interdependency between people and countries and if you destroy others than you might destroy yourself. This reality should be taught in schools, proper dialogue, compromising, environmental concerns are not restricted to boundaries.

A sadhu in India might look deprived but he is calm and content. In order to get a happy life, calm mind is important and in turn to acquire this, jealousy/anger and strong attachment has to be removed in one's life. Strong compassion towards others is again the answer. Questions which were asked by the audience and answered by His Holiness Dalai Lama

Q. Do you want violence to be used to free Tibet.?

A. No, no violence at all, Live peacefully side-by-side, avoid violence.

Q. Do you know more than others?

A. In our discussions earlier with Desmond Tutu, we did not know that this is an ice-arena (PNE) and hockey players make such a lot of money, were in the wrong profession.

Q. Do you feel sad sometimes?

A. There has to be an analytical meditation, look at it at a different angle, be positive. News from

Tibet makes me sad but I've had new opportunity, meet different people, scientists, politicians and Desmond Tutu. If I was still in Tibet, I might have been more orthodox, conservative. Everything is relative-Buddhist point of view.

Q. What do you think of terrorism?

A. I think Desmond Tutu can answer better cause of his work with "Truth and Re-conciliation. (Archbishop Desmond Tutu: We know terrorism is evil but we are obligated to find root causes of it)

Q. Are you afraid of death, why or why not?

A. As per Buddhist point of you, at this time connection between body and mind is stopped. No regrets If you had a meaningful life. Right attitude. Birth is foundation of death.

Q. How can we stop worrying?

A. Look at life at different angles and be realistic.

Q. Why are they no women Dai Lama's

A. There are senior positions held by women in the Dharamsala. But who knows a time will come when one might be selected.

NATIVE CHIEF MERCREDI FOLLOWING MAHATMA GANDHI'S NON-VIOLENCE WAY

by Prakash V. Joshi
As published in The Link, October 30, 1996

The Assembly of First Nations (AFN) hosted a conference on non-violence in Vancouver October 10 through October 11, 1996 at the Squamish Recreation Center.

(from left) Dr. N. Radha Krishnan, Grand Chief Ovide Mercredi, Dr. Devendra Kumar, Prakash (Writer) and wife Darshan Joshi

Native Chief Mercredi Following Mahatma Gandhi's Non-Violence Way

BY PRAKASH JOSHI

(VANCOUVER) - The Assembly of First Nations (AFN) hosted a conference on non-violence in Vancouver October 10 through October 11, 1996 at the Squamish Recreation Center. Chiefs and delegates travelled from across Canada to attend. Two special guests from India were invited. The conference was organized following the events of the summer of 1995, when two highly publicized arm confrontation took place, (Gustafsan and Ippawash) following the crisis at Oka.

As the three day conference wrapped up, the theme of the conference, "First nations traditions of non-violence" was again echoed by the Grand chief of Assembly of First Nations, Ovide Mercredi. He saw non-violence as the only real solution for his peoples' hurt, historical injuries, and discrimination. "Non-violence is about love and healing, when you are calm in your approach, you give medicine. When you are angry and violent you give poison. This conference has to say to the Canadian government and the rest of the people that we are and always were non-violent people."

At the end of last year, Mercredi made a spiritual journey to India, accompanied by Dr. N. Radha Krishnan. For three weeks, he learned about the history of the Non-violent movement. Dr. Krishnan, a world authority on the subject of Mahatma Gandhi's philosophy, saw a sincere leader who was totally convinced to resolve the conflict through peaceful means.

Dr. Krishnan who was invited by Mercredi to speak at the conference mentioned about Gandhiji's effort to unite the two biggest religious groups during the freedom movement in India. The spokesmen for N-Y-M (Native Youth Movement), reminded the native leaders about the importance of unity amongst native leaders.

The final sessions of the conference day were mainly dedicated to the youth delegates. It was both difficult and painful as each took the microphone to express their feelings.

Finally, holding hands and consoling each other, the youths made an emotional plea, "Will work for love. Non-violence is love."

Dr. Devendra Kumar, Director of Center of Science for villages in India, also invited by The Grand Chief, spoke on current research being carried out in appropriate technologies for sustainable development along Gandhian lines tion to another," he said.

On Friday night (October 10th 1996) at traditional Squamish feast I witnessed the similarities in cultures, respect of elders and guests, prayers to the creator, just a subtle difference in "arti", colorful costumes and dances with a bhangra style drum beat. As Roy Naidu, tabla accompaniment and myself went on the stage to perform one of Gandhiji's favorite bhajans, one of the native performer jokingly, but with respect said "it is time for the real Indians to perform."

Chief Ovide Mercredi knelt down and sang a Cree prayer, as he burned a braid of sweetgrass, in a traditional ceremony performed at Ma-

Grand Chief Mercredi with Squamish Nation Performers

to help improve village life. Commenting on the youth workshop, Dr. Devendra Kumar said that he had never heard such deep, clear, feelings of expression. "This deep spiritual concepts will be passed on from one generation hatma Gandhi's cremation ground. This was in India. He paid special tribute to the person whose teachings he hopes will bring a peaceful dialogue between The Canadian Government and The First Nations.

Raj Mohan Gandhi Carries on The Legacy of His Grandfather

by Prakash V. Joshi
As published in The Link Newspaper, November 4, 1995

A letter from Prime Minister Jean Chretien welcomed "The Bridge Builder", Raj Mohan Gandhi (grandson of Mahatma) to Canada.

Farewell to Rev. Pandurang Shastri Athavale

Flint Center for Performing Arts at DeAnza College, San Francisco by Prakash V. Joshi March 2004

In May of 1997 when I stood at the gates of the beautiful In May of 1997 when I stood at the gates of the beautiful

Westminster Abbey in London, England thousands of followers of Shri Pandurang Shastri, 'Dada' were full of joy and excitement as their spiritual leader who had taught them to see "God in all people" were about to witness a historic moment, Dadaji was about to be presented with the Templeton award by Prince Philip for his outstanding work, 'For Progress in Religion' The prestigious award was valued at $1.21 million.

But this time it was different, outside the DeAnza College, in the garden with a water fountain in the middle plus a band playing, there were thousands of followers, mostly of Indian descent waiting this time in silence to say goodbye to 'Dadaji'(elder brother), their spiritual leader who had turned their lives around. They had come from as far as New Zealand and Fiji but mostly representing The West Zone Swadhyay Kendra, Vancouver (BC), Seattle, Portland, Sacramento, Los Angeles, San Diego and San Francisco.

Dadaji passed away on October 25th last year at 83. His daughter,

Didiji (elder sister) has been traveling with his ashes around the world to give followers, in millions now, an opportunity to memorialize him.

Westminster Abbey in London, England thousands of followers of Shri Pandurang Shastri, 'Dada' were full of joy and excitement as their spiritual leader who had taught them to see "God in all people" were about to witness a historic moment, Dadaji was about to be presented with the Templeton award by Prince Philip for his outstanding work, 'For Progress in Religion' The prestigious award was valued at $1.21 million.

But this time it was different, outside the DeAnza College, in the garden with a water fountain in the middle plus a band playing, there were thousands of followers, mostly of Indian descent waiting this time in silence to say goodbye to 'Dadaji'(elder brother), their spiritual leader who had turned their lives around. They had come from as far as New Zealand and Fiji but mostly representing The West Zone Swadhyay Kendra, Vancouver (BC), Seattle, Portland, Sacramento, Los Angeles, San Diego and San Francisco.

Dadaji passed away on October 25th last year at 83. His daughter,

Didiji (elder sister) has been traveling with his ashes around the world to give followers, in millions now, an opportunity to memorialize him.

The memorial started at 10:15 on the morning of March 13th 2004, with the arrival of Didiji as she brought forward an urn containing his ashes. As the band played, 83 doves were set free representing one for each year of his life. As they flew off, the eyes of the crowd turned to the clear sky witnessing yet another moving experience, a plane circling above with a banner, 'Tava Chaha Parinam HogaDadaji', 'Your wish will come true-Dadaji'.

As the Indian inspirational music played, the crowd followed Didiji and invited dignitaries into the theatre lined up with Dadaji's photos and his popular sayings.

Children under 12 years were guided by the volunteers to a special room.

Once seated Didiji paid respect to the ashes by lighting a lamp and garlanding them with flowers and Dadaji's favourite scarf.

The dignitaries who spoke included Hon. Governor Brown who compared Dadaji's work with Mother

Teresa whereby how just one individual's spirit had touched lives of millions. The Indian Consulate

General, Hon. Mr. Mishra reminded the crowd of the Padma Bhushan awarded to Dadaji by The President of India in 1995. Congressman, Hon. Mike Honda praised his tireless work in trying to create one family, "A family of human beings". Jagmohanji representing the sikh community made special mention of Dadaji paying respects to holy "Guru Granth Sahib" in 1997 at Nanded. (In the words of the holy priest, Avtar Singh, at Nanded Gurudwara, India, (Such welcome as bestowed upon Dada has never been given to anyone, even to a prime minister or any dignitary").

Didiji often overcoming with emotions and tears briefly described Dadajis work and showed a video, emphasizing the importance of the continuation of his work even though it had been a tragic blow to all the followers. The video ended with the 40,000 youths in Baruch shouting, "We will, we will", promising Dada to continue with his work.

As about 2,400 followers lined up to view the ashes, a team of men in white recited slokas from the Bhagavad Gita, holy Hindu book.

Born on October 19, 1920 in Raigad District, of a Brahmin family, Dadaji as a child hated to see cast differences. He founded the Swadhyaya (Self- awareness) movement in 1958 which preaches that barrier of cast, gender and religion must be transcend in order to recognize the true equality of all people. He has transformed nearly hundred thousand villages in India, carrying on mass movement bestowing dignity on the underprivileged, bringing social reform through participant toil for the poor without any expectation of personal gain. His spiritual base being the Bhagavad Gita describing his work as "Apounasheya Laxhmi", impersonal wealth. He was awarded Magsaysay Award in 1996 for community leadership comprising of $50,000.

The Ramon Magsaysay Award Foundation honours outstanding Asians every year. The Award is named after Philippine President Ramon Magsaysay who died in a plane crash in 1957.

Dadaji's followers number in millions worldwide and about fifteen thousand in America.

As Ruskin Seth, a follower and a resident of San Francisco said, " We are part of history, our children and grandchildren will be very proud to know that we were in presence of a such great person."

"It took hundreds of years for people to realize the greatness of Christ so it's not important that there are still plenty who don't know of Dadaji's great work, it is up to us to stay focused and carry on with what he taught us", said Mahesh Shah.

Dinesh Patel added, "I really didn't realize his true worth in India, when I was young but coming to United States, after listening to Dadas 'pravachans' and going on Bhakti -pheri has had a profound change on me and my family. It has brought respect, peace, love and harmony in this sometime difficult the materialistic world".

Yatin Parikh spoke of the the fond memories and some very hard times they had incurred during the first bhakti-pheri (devotional visits) to Vancouver in the cold winter of 1996. Not only had they got lost in a new city but couldn't find a single motel/hotel to spend the night in due to the football game. They searched till two O'clock at night and then decided to spend the night in the car. Fortunately, they didn't have to spend the whole night in the car. Total strangers to me but it was their thoughts and the fact that they had come all the way from San Francisco in the name of brotherhood which had inspired me to go to Westminister Abbey in 1997 and find out more about Dadaji, as a reporter. But this time I had come to San Francisco, not as a reporter but as a member of the Swadhyay Pariwar, to pay homage to a humanitarian whose simple humble message " of seeing God in all" had a profound effect on me.

Prakash Vinod Joshi, AScT, Eng.L
Senior Materials Engineering Technologist

DAVID SUZUKI - THE AUTOBIOGRAPHY

by Prakash V. Joshi

NEWS

David Suzuki – The Autobiography

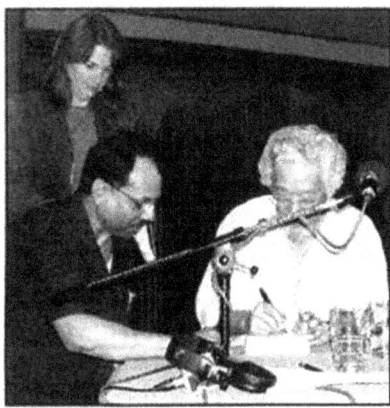

By Prakash V. Joshi, AScT, Limited Licensee (Engineering)
Senior Materials Engineering Technologist

I have always admired the Environmental work carried out by Dr. David Suzuki (Not forgetting the ever popular documentary T.V. series "The Nature of Things") plus the initiatives he's taken towards "Paths to Peace", so when I was informed by CBC Radio that I had won two tickets to the CBC Radio Studio One Book Club with him on May 7th, 2006, my wife and I were simply delighted. The limited capacity at the studio of 100 people meant, you were required to write a 100 word essay on Dr. Suzuki to qualify for a sit.

As noted by the positive interaction between Dr. Suzuki and the audience, the "die-hard-fans" were once again ready for yet another fantastic treat, all eager to ask questions and have their newly purchased book, " David Suzuki – The Autobiography ", autographed by him. The session started with Dr. Suzuki mentioning about his childhood dreams to visit the wildebeest stampede in Africa and the Amazon Forests/Indians. He had visited the Amazon tribe called "The Kaiakan" and with help of the Indian chief, Paiakan helped to prevent the construction of a dam which would have destroyed the Kaiakan village by flooding it. Seventy thousand dollars were raised for this project. He narrated a passage from his book.

He highlighted the closeness to his parents by citing examples. His mother, when he was young would never scold him but in fact encourage him as he would come back home, dirty after playing frequently in the swamp, exhibiting insects he'd caught. His father who had only completed grade 12 was both his admirer and critic of his work. He would caution him and say, "If I don't understand what you're saying how do you expect others to understand". This was meant for him to make his presentations simpler and easy to understand. He adored and respected his dad. His strong feelings of being an "outsider" in the country he was born, Canada were mainly due to the time he spend, when he was young, in the internment Japanese camp during World war II. "It was my first experience of alienation and isolation, and it gave me a life long sense of an outsider". He also read another passage from the book regarding his father's last days eloquently speaking about old age and death. The proud father who used to say, " You are what you do, not what you say".

The two hour session was not enough to quench the thirst of the audience asking questions which included concerns on the, Climate change, Kyoto Protocol, Forest/Marine ecosystems, Energy crisis, Nuclear Power stations, David Suzuki Foundation and some of local environmental projects.

Not to give away too much of the above presentation as it will be on air shortly, the show was taped for broadcast on North by Northwest in two parts over one weekend: Part One on May 27, between 8 and 9 am and Part Two May 28th, 8 to 9 am both on CBC Radio (690 on am dial in Vancouver).

[David Suzuki is an acclaimed geneticist and environmentalist, the founder and chair of the David Suzuki Foundation, and author of more than forty books, including The Sacred Balance (coauthored with Amanda McConnell)' Tree (coauthored with Wayne Grady), and Good News for change (coauthored with Holly Dressel). He has been named a companion of the order of Canada and holds eighteen honorary degrees from institutions in Canada, United States, and Australia.

Impressive Ceremony Honours Spiritual Leader With Templeton Award

By Prakash Joshi

As I stood at the gates of the beautiful Westminster Abbey, in

Prakash Joshi

the typical chilly London winds, continuing my press-credentials with security guards, I couldn't help but feel really lucky to be able to attend the ceremony, and many hundreds were disappointed, to be able to be there in person, to honour 'Dada'. For example, nearly a thousand were applied from the United States to come but only three hundred were issued invitations. This was also true in other countries whereby in India, only fifty were allowed and hundreds couldn't make it even though many had acquired visas. The security was at the peak, as H.R.H. Prince

Philip was in attendance, presenting the award.

The award ceremonies originally began in 1972 by the renowned global investor, Sir John Templeton. The prize is given each year to living persons who have shown extraordinary originality in advancing humankind's understanding of God and/or love. The prize value of about 750,000 pounds sterling, about $1.21 million, is the world's largest monetary award. Some of the nine judges for the prize included George Bush, former President of United States and The Reverend Nichiko Niwano, President, Risoho KoseiKai, Japan. Shri Pandurang Shastri Athvale is the fourth person from India to receive the prize, his predecessors being Mother Teresa (1973), Sister Pilai Vattom Ittan (1975), and Baba Amte 1990 (jointly with Charles Birch of Australia).

Westminster Abbey, an impressive Gothic Church of England is the traditional site of coronations and contains the tombs of many English monarch, states-man and national heroes.

The ceremony started at 6:30 pm, and as the organ played on, 'Dada', in a wheelchair pushed in procession, accompanied by his adopted daughter, 'Didi'. He was followed by John Templeton Jr. and Dr. John Templeton Jr. accompanied by a procession of previous recipients and of the Judges of the 1997 prize. Lastly, his Royal Highness, Prince Philip, Duke of Edinburgh, proceeded to the lantern. The Reverend Colin Semper (Canon of West-

minster) greeted the guests.

Dr. John M. Templeton, Jr., President of the Templeton Foundation Inc. addressed the guests and described the work of the foundation and its history. He said, "It is a special coincidence that the recipient of the award this year has travelled from India as did the first recipient, Mother Teresa." In describing the work of Shri Pandurang Shastri he added, "We gather together to honour one who has changed the condition of living for millions of villagers throughout India. He is one, who by his faith in God, has realized spiritual and ma-

terial progress for these millions in their daily lives. He is one who represents the tradition of India's classical learning and what is best in social knowledge available in other traditions. His philosophy is based on total and absolute faith in God and service to God through service to others. He continued, "That person, whom we honour tonight, is Mr. Shri Pandurang Shastri Athavale. Mr. Athavale, was born in Maharashtra, in October, 1920. In honouring his life's work, the citation for his award reads: "Motivated by deep commitment to the service of God.

Mr. Athavale has enabled several million Indian villagers to achieve a better social status through the spiritual revolution that began in 1956."

With the help of a cane and 'Didi' by his side, Dada walked to the centre of the sacrarium. His royal Highness, Duke of Edinburgh also, moved to the centre of the sacrarium where he presented 'Dada', the John Templeton Award.

It gives great pleasure to see Shri Pandurang Shastri Athavale's acceptance speech in its entirety, especially with brothers and sisters who were not able to attend the ceremony. The speech was initiated by 'Dada', continued by Didi (as indicated) and then concluded by Dada'.

The Link on such an historical occasion.

Crowds lining up outside the Westminster Abbey before the award ceremony

VISIT TO MT. CURRIE

STRUGGLE OF ST'AT'IMC FIRST NATION PEOPLE

On March 3rd, 2007 I visited The Mt. Currie reservation, past Whistler/Pemberton. The three-hour bus ride from Vancouver takes you through the most beautiful coastal scenic route in the world.

I had been invited by Bill Chu amongst others, 56 in all on the yearly trip to meet with St'at'imc First Nation people at Mt. Currie. Bill Chu represents "Canadians for Reconciliation", a peaceful nonpartisan grassroots movement committed to developing a new relation with aboriginal people, one that signifies a deep apology for past injustices, a willingness to honor truth now and a resolve to embrace each other in the new millennium.

On May 2nd, 2000, members of the St'at'imc nation and their allies established a permanent camp near Melvin Creek, located off Highway 99 between Mt. Currie/Pemberton and Lillooet, in the southern interior region of B.C.

Known as Suitikalh, the St'at'imc winter spirit of the area the camp was set up to stop government and corporate plans to build a $500 million all-season ski and recreation resort in an untouched Alpine Mountain area.

Part of the Cayoosh Mountain Range, the region is a transition zone from the coast to the interior. It is a habitat Grizzly bears, cougars, bobcat, wolverine, deer, hawks, owls and many other small animals. It also contains one of the largest herds of Mountain Goats now remaining in North America.

The area has been occupied and used by the St'at'imc for as long as 10,000 years, following the retreat of the glacial period which carved out the steep –sided valleys and jagged mountain tops.

Along with the food gathering, the area was also used by shamans who went to the mountains for purification, spiritual renewal and training. These traditions continue to be practiced today at Sutikalh, where people come to gather foods, medicine, pure fresh water, and to participate in cultural and spiritual activities.

As we huddled together, in the basement of the house belonging to the elder, grandma/mom,

Georgina Nelson, quietly listening to the above brief history and struggle of the St'at'mic people, Rosalin Sam continued, also citing some personal tragedies. As a young innocent child, she was torn from her family and taken to a residential school. She was punished by the nuns for speaking her native language and sent to a cold closet and made to sit on the cold floor on her knees for hours, hence the arthritis problem in her legs at this age. She mentioned about a friend she had in the school, sexually abused by the priest, and becoming pregnant. The child, aborted was buried in the nearby grave but her friend soon became suicidal and died at the tender age of thirteen.

"To this day the area remains unceded, unsurrendered St'at'imc territory, in which neither Canada nor BC have legal or moral authority to govern, claim territory or even carry out business."

Rosalin Sam, a Lil'watool of St'at'ime, is a mother and grandmother working to protect the St'at'me territory-for the sake of the ancestors who fought for it at the cost of their blood, and for the future for her grandchild's grandchildren.

The session ended with a beautiful native prayer song and we were then invited upstairs for lunch. As I thanked the host, elder Georgina Nelson, her son Alvin Nelson mentioned about her mother's recent visit to Uganda, attending a conference, Women's forum-'Another World.' This was a very pleasant surprise, as we shared stories about my birth - place, Uganda.

As the sun came out, everyone gathered around the log-fire, in the front yard, except for a few kids who couldn't miss the opportunity, playing in the snow. With a creek running nearby and the snowcapped mountains in the distance, the peaceful tranquility was broken by yet another sad incidence that an elder described when he was young and spent time at a residential school. The priest/teacher asked his name, as a ten-year innocent boy he replied and gave his native name, he was slapped and asked again. He repeated and gave his native name rather than the Christian name he was given, once again he was slapped resulting in an everlasting deafness in one of his ears. He did well in school and completed UBC and excelled in sports, equal to good football players during his time. He cautioned his listeners not to look down on the natives they see on Vancouver's skid row, often it's due to the abuse and suffering caused in the time at residential schools, by both their parents and them. He termed this a genocide, comparing it to the suffering of Jews during the times of Hitler. His out-cry and on-going fight and struggle with the authorities to preserve the pristine valleys which his ancestors had lived in harmony with for thousands of years was supported by several environmental groups like Society Promoting Environmental Conservation (SPEC), The Western Canada Wilderness Committee (WCWC) and Sierra Club and even former government biologist.

The afternoon bus ride took us through the winding compacted dirt road, through the reservation, once stopping for herds of horses blocking the road and then ended with a brisk walk on the sandy beaches of Lake Lillooet. The trip ended with gifts and a three-hour ride back home to Vancouver with everlasting memories of people who had respected the land, learnt to share rather than take and an ongoing suffering.

"When you travel between Mt. Currie and Lillooet, there are countless breathtaking country scenes, with all of the beautiful colors of Mother Nature's palette. This is a place for wildlife to roam; a place where the stream water is pure enough to drink; a place where you can breathe in the fresh air and, on a clear night, you can see all the stars in the sky; a place that was made by the Creator with all creatures in mind. All of this exists within the St'at'imc Nation. We cannot see it destroyed for the sake of the almighty dollar. Money will disappear quickly, but the land will be there for thousands of years to come."

Prakash Vinod Joshi, ASCT, Eng.L
Senior Materials Engineering Technologist
(Web Site: www.pvjoshi.ca)

India – Tibet has a Guru-Disciple relationship – His Holiness Dalai Lama

by Prakash V. Joshi
As published in The Link Newspaper, September 18, 2006

At the age of 71, His Holiness Dalai Lama, was still full of energy and humor after a long trip when he made his first stop at the Vancouver City Hall. It was his fourth trip to Vancouver. In welcoming his Holiness, Vancouver Mayor Sam Sullivan and the trustees from the Dalai Lama centre for Peace and Education, respectfully acknowledged the fact that they were standing on the traditional territory of the Coast Salish people.

They then thanked his Holiness for blessing Vancouver with his presence. The reason for the visit was the official inauguration of the Centre and the launching of a series public dialogues. The purpose of the dialogues was to provide a unique opportunity to join with the Dalai Lama and leading global thinkers in considering issues of universal responsibility and compassion as a foundation for peace.

In response, His Holiness gave his thanks for a fine welcome. He also stressed the importance of multiculturalism, and gave his vision of the whole world as one entity/body with cities made up of people from all faiths and cultures living in harmony in this vision priority would be given to both finding a common purpose among people and "trying to preserve each individual identity".

The first question from the media was about his honorary Canadian Citizenship. In responding he pointed out the similarities between snowy Tibet and Canada. With much humor he indicated to Mayor Sullivan and the media that he was very interested in finding out more about his newly acquired rights and privileges as an honorary citizen but not the duties and responsibilities as he was going to be in the city for a very short stay. He mentioned the few thousand Tibetans now living in Canada and said they were very happy here. He thanked Canada for accepting him as a "brother".

The second question from the media was about his health as his doctors had advised him against any travel and recommended a complete rest. His Holiness mentioned that he recently had a bad cough with fever and there was a concern that he might have TB. However, anti-biotics, a complete three/four weeks of rest, and studying and reading scriptures helped him to overcome that.

The Canadian Press reporter inquired about the stand that The Peoples Republic of China had taken, suggesting that Canadian government granting him an honorary citizenship might harm relations between the two countries. His Holiness replied, "You should judge yourself". He elaborated on the issue, mentioning some past incidences, which had caused serious protests, and he was really sorry about them and for the inconveniences that it had caused but later there had been no consequences and said, "but hopefully it's not my mistake".

A lady from the Chinese Cable T.V. inquired about the purpose of his visit. In replying he said with a smile, "I was invited, very simple". He cited two important reasons for his visit. One to promote "human values" and secondly to promote a "rich harmony".

Human values included, "improving inner qualities, sustaining life, like the affection of a mother towards a child, feeling of care, which was not due to any religious factor but a biological need and this

experience is the foundation, even though 71 years old, I still feel the mother's care which brings "inner peace", this feeling, others have the potential to have. As the brain develops with intelligence, increase of short-sightedness takes place due to the influence of the environment, leading to anger, aggressiveness, jealousy- the basic values are submerged. The time has come, through listening, education and research efforts to sustain our basic instinct and be more peaceful and compassionate towards others, through dialogues."

Rich Harmony: "media has an important role to play, I admire free media, and it should have a long nose like the elephant to search for the truth. The public has the right to know the reality –Honest truthful reporting. The initiatives and the interest of having a peace centre were first discussed during the last visit with assistance of Victor Chan and University of British Columbia. In the past religious institutes were responsible for ethics and spirituality. In modern times spirituality and family values have declined. The educational system should take full responsibility of moral ethics and promote love, compassion and forgiveness. Highly educated, intelligent millionaires are still not happy - why? Mental peace enhances the immune system and thus prevents illness." Therefore, the main reason to come here is to develop Happy Communities".

A woman from CBC T.V. questioned the need for yet another centre in Vancouver to facilitate learning of Tai Chi, a library and a cinema. His Holiness the Dalai Lama clarified the need for a centre to assist in coordinating work in education, research and dialogue, a place to make you a better and a compassionate human being.

When asked by the media whether the Tibetans were oppressed by the Chinese in Tibet, His Holiness encourage them to go and find it out themselves, "Go there and spend some time there, not only in towns but country-side as well, take a translator with you. The information received seems to indicate, the local Tibetans expressed sadness, even some of the local Chinese in Tibet agree with that." A gentleman from the Vancouver Sun asked about whether the centre would have any connection with freeing Tibet. His Holiness stressed that it was strictly educational and non-political. He confessed that his "non-independence stand" had not been readily accepted by all the Tibetans and in fact Tibetan Youth Organization had been very critical and seek complete independence.

In responding to the question from a reporter from Channel 'M', regarding the effect of cultural and traditional values on an average Tibetan due to the recent Chinese railway link to Tibet, his Holiness spoke about the population growth of Chinese in Tibet. In the Tibetan town of Lhasa, the Tibetans are a minority. Their population is 100,000 as compared to the Chinese which is 200,000. Chinese being the official language, it is more frequently spoken. Plus music/food has an influence on the young Tibetan.

"Either intentional or non –intentional, it's a cultural genocide".

His Holiness had grave concerns about the construction going on in his country. The depleting snow caps due to global warming and the scarcity of drinking water is a problem. This melting water is the source of numerous major rivers which feed water to India, China, Cambodia, Pakistan, Bangladesh, and Laos. He encouraged seeking the advice of scientists and environmentalist before the commencement of any construction projects.

I was always interested in the influence of Indians on the Tibetans living in India and vice versa. As I introduced myself to his Holiness, at the end of the media QA session, to ask the last question, I made special mention of the fact that I indeed had something in common with him, I too had to flee from my country of birth, Uganda and now am living in the best country in the world. It was our turn to make him laugh for a change. His hearty laugh once again penetrated into our skins, especially mine. To my surprise he made a very bold statement saying that he had often mentioned to his fellow Tibetans and Mongolian friends that a thousand years ago when Buddhism first came to their land, the natives were "barbarians". He related India and Tibet having a relationship of a teacher/guru to a disciple/student. He considered India having a model democracy. Though the Sunni and Shia Muslims in the Middle East showed differences there, in India they all lived happily together. He highlighted the origins of the Sanskrit word Ahinsa meaning non-violence and non-injury. The Tibetan youth brought up in India was more of a "Tibetan" than his counterpart in Tibet due to the Chinese influence. Buddhism had definitely aroused the interest of some of the Indian youth and the way of life definitely has lots to offer. As the session ended, he came around to the journalists to shake their hands, he shook mine and asked me my Indian origins, and I replied, "Gujarat, the land of Mahatma Gandhi". "But are you a vegetarian?' he asked. I said, "of course" and he smiled and walked slowly away.

I would again have the pleasure of seeing His Holiness, at two other occasions, though this time from a distance when he would participate in a dialogue with leading scientists, organized by the Center and the UBC Institute of Mental Health at the Orpheum Theatre on Saturday the 9th of September. The theme: Happiness and Stress as Determinants of Mental Health.

"The basic sources of happiness are good heart, compassion and love, if we have this mental attitude, even if we are surrounded by hostility, we feel little disturbance. On the other hand, we lack compassion and our mental state is filled with anger or hatred we will not have peace."

During the afternoon session, on the same day His Holiness spoke on "Cultivating Happiness" at the GM Place. The crowd was treated to a Tibetan culture through dances, music and a children's choir.

Around 12,000 people witnessed the Dalai Lama receive his honorary Canadian citizenship from

Immigration Minister, Monte Solberg. Only two other people have been granted the honorary citizenship, Nelson Mandela of South Africa and Swedish diplomat Raoul Wallenberg, who rescued many European Jews during Holocaust.

Two years ago I had the opportunity to write about the historic visit of His Holiness the Dalai Lama with Archbishop Desmond Tutu and Professor Shirin Ebadi, the three Nobel Peace Prize recipients. In the hearts of British Columbians, His Holiness the Dalai Lama still remains a spiritual superstar but according his Holiness, "I'm just a simple Buddhist monk".

Prakash Vinod Joshi, AScT, Eng.L
Senior Materials Engineering Technologist
Metro Group

Reconciling Communities on Canada Day

by Prakash V. Joshi
July 1, 2006

On June 27th I was invited with others to Bill Chu's home. It was the first time I had ever met him and his wife Sylvia but I was impressed by their humbleness. Over a cup of tea Bill described his vision about getting not only the Chinese community but all communities to participate in a 'Parade of Reconciliation' on July 1st, 2006, commemorating Canada Day.

The backdrop was the federal government's parliamentary apology and redress for the Chinese Head Tax survivors and those directly affected on June 22, 2006. The current government provided an official redress to end historic injustice to Chinese-Canadians.

The parade started with a rally at Victory Square. Speakers included Bill Chu, founder of Canadians for Reconciliation, Bill Siksay MP for Burnaby North, Peter Ladner, Vancouver City Councilor and pastors Tama WardBalisky and Wayne Lo.

Bill Chu gave a brief history of the rampant discrimination suffered by the early Chinese immigrants: more than 24 anti-Chinese pieces of legislation proposed in British Columbia (1878-1913), the removal of Chinese students from classrooms, the banning of Chinese from public swimming, the restricted seating in theatres and entrance to universities, the inability to own houses, etc.... One of the purposes of the parade was to symbolically reverse the 1907 anti-Chinese immigration parade that turned into an ugly riot where a mob of 9000 ransacked Vancouver Chinatown with some Chinese jumped into False Creek to escape harm. 'What we need most now is to educate the public about how Canadians treated minorities in the past. Without that, Canadians will miss the log in their eyes and the need for reconciliation.' He again stressed the importance of not to dwell only on the government's past injustices but to educate the public so that citizens would take ownership of past communal discrimination and walk together for spiritual reconciliation.

The pastors provided a moving message that apology and reconciliation is important in relation building.MP Bill Siksay apologized on behalf of his ancestors and family who benefited from collecting the taxes and emphasized the need and the importance of the parade. Councilor Ladner voiced the City support for the work of reconciliation. The speeches ended with the Chinese and non-Chinese coming together in a spirit of mutual embrace. Then the parade started at Victory Square and ended at the Mennonites Seniors home in China town. Sweets in red envelopes embossed with the words Peace and Joy were distributed to store owners along the way, as well as amongst the seniors. The walk was also punctuated with a stop at every city block in China town. All participants lined up along the curb on opposite sides of Pender Street and observed a minute of silence to symbolically express their deep sorrow over the hate and discrimination that occurred in the past. At the end of the parade, participants entered the senior home and had an opportunity to celebrate the purpose of the parade with seniors including a Mrs. Wan who is 105 years old.

Prakash Joshi, AScT, Limited Licensee (Engineering)
Senior Materials Engineering Technologist

UVIC Honours Miria Matembe of Uganda

by Prakash Vinod Joshi, AScT, Eng.L

Senior Materials Engineering Technologist
Published in "The Link Newspaper" on Saturday June 30, 2007

On June 9th 2007, University of Victoria awarded honorary degree at a convocation to Hon. Miria Matembe of Uganda. As a member of the Pan-African Parliament she also served as a chairperson of its Committee on Rules. As a former Ugandan Minister of Ethics and Integrity from 1998 to 2003, she formulated the government's policy on corruption and helped set standards of ethics for professionals in public office. In 2002, she published a memoir entitled "Gender, Politics and Constitution Making in Uganda", documenting her experiences and bringing gender issues to the forefront of national politics.

To celebrate her achievements and accomplishments, Ms. Matembe's sister, Margaret Mubanda (Treasurer of UCNA, Ugandan- Canadian Association of Canada) and John Halani of Tropicana Hotel, Vancouver, organized a reception on June 11th, 2007 at The Samosa Gardens, in Vancouver.

In answering questions after her presentation regarding her role as a member of Pan-African Parliament she gave a short history of the organization, noting the origins of OAU, Organization of African Union which was formed during the colonial period whose primary objective was to fight aparthied. As the African countries gained independence Pan-African Parliament was formed to facilitate the effective implementation of the policies and objectives of the OAU and, ultimately the African Union. Primarily, to promote the principles of human rights and democracy in Africa. She laughed and admitted that African countries are slow in accepting democracy but eventually coming around as leaders like late President Nyerere of Tanzania and President Mandela of South Africa are setting examples to other leaders to step down, give up their "thrones", hold elections which she said, "looked positive though they might be rigged," she said jokingly.

On gender issues, her greatest victories, she said was a constitutionally mandated quota of at least 28.8 % women in the national parliament, but she felt that the system had brought about complacency and in fact an impediment to real progress for women in Uganda. They regard the quota system as a sign of privilege on the part of government and are therefore unwilling to raise their voice. The women's right to own property is still a burning issue and the government has been reluctant to pass laws.

"Men, she said, had created enough wars and caused enough violence that it is time to have women assist in creating peace in the world. Men and women both participate in making a baby and takes that takes only a few minutes. Then God made the woman responsible for the human creation and nurturing and bringing up so it is but natural to have a woman be part of the decision making concerning human life."

Commenting on Aids rate in Uganda, she proudly claimed had dropped from 15% of the population in 1990's to current low of 6%. This was done mainly due to the local efforts rather than any help from outside. In 1986 when NRM (National Resistance Movement) came to power, lead by Yoweri Musweni, after years of brutal wars and genocide, by dictators like Idi Amin Dada, there was hope of democracy and the government was very receptive of women participation. Miria Matembe was one of the two women lawyers appointed in putting the new constitution together. Matembe confirmed, "It was like eating the hand that fed you," Her last straw with the government was when President Museweni advised her to disregard the two five-year terms for the president as outlined in the constitution so that he could stay on.

No matter what the differences were between the two, she explained she supported President Musweni's policies in Northern Uganda. She confirmed that the situation is getting better but the psychological impact on the children torn from their families, raped, used as soldiers for last two decades by LRA (Lord Resistance Army) and it's leader Joseph Kony would take long to heal. The Ugandan Government and LRA are now talking, so that's a good start. There was no discussion about the recent riots which happened in Uganda when a local Indian Industrialist decided to cut-down the pristine Mabira Forest to farm sugar cane. There was an uproar amongst the native Ugandans and an Indian called Devag Rawal (NRI) was stoned to death. The press often did not mention the two Africans who died, too in the riot. As a Ugandan Indian refugee, expelled by Idi Amin Dada in 1970's I was extremely moved by the gesture shown by President Musweni who sent a delegation to India, headed by Internal affairs minister, Ruhakana Rugunda to personally convey the condolences of the Ugandan people to the Indian government and to the victim's parents. There was also a compensation of 400,000 rupees awarded to Devag's parents. This tremendous gesture by the President was once again a commitment to welcome Indians in Uganda and safeguard their interests. This type of gesture was the first of his kind and really not evident in the world, today.

Prakash Vinod Joshi, AScT, Eng.L
Senior Materials Engineering Technologist (The above article was published in "The Link Newspaper" on Saturday June 30, 2007)

Conclusion-Canada

1. Children

In California and Alaska parents pay a fine to schools if they do not carry out their duties or are not responsible; for example, at the kindergarten level, if they bring children late to school. Parents complain about children not doing well, often placing the blame on the teachers. By the same token, what do we do as a society if the children, at a very tender age, are abandoned by their parents or by one of the parents and a community that looks the other way?

2. Seniors

As our children grow up in this country, we both hope they will be able to pick up a few things that we have been able to share with them. We had a few seniors living in our neighborhood, some in their 90s, and during winter snowfall I would ask the kids to shovel the snow from their driveways. As the seniors tried to compensate them with money, I would not allow the kids to except it. I wanted them to help without excepting to be rewarded, just like my grandfather had done. My uppermost concern in life is the materialistic society that we are living in and building for the future for our children. Money seems to be the most important among all the priorities and nothing else seems to be more important, even at the cost of destroying this beautiful planet.

As I was growing up and went to school, the rich and the poor all wore the same clothes, the uniform. The focus was on education and not on "brand name" clothes. The students don't need any more distractions than they are already bombarded with on television.

3. Environment

As we built a tree house together, I reinforced the idea of building it in such a way as to cause the least damage to the tree and preserve the natural environment surrounding it. So as it was built I made sure that the least amount of branches were cut and fewest possible nails used.

This meant having a collar on each of the two trees and lumber nailed on to them going from one tree to the other, thus acting like the trusses for the floor. The tree house had branches going right through it. In simple ways I tried to make the children realize the importance of the ways nature makes it liveable for us on this planet; trees taking in carbon dioxide and giving back oxygen, the roots preventing erosion and insects helping with pollination.

On CBC radio the kids and some technicians from the Environmental division of the company I worked with suddenly heard my voice echoing from the radio, asking a question to David Suzuki regarding the status of nuclear stations in Canada. This was in reference to an article I had recently read in the National Geographic Magazine, "20 years since the Chernobyl Nuclear disaster in which the fallout had 400 times more radioactivity than released at Hiroshima." David Suzuki alluded to the high cost of building nuclear stations and the maintenance cost. Most of the nuclear facilities were based in Ontario. Also, he spoke about the high cost and the dilemma of getting rid of the radioactive waste. Lastly, after the 9/11 tragedy, he cautioned about a nuclear station being taken over by terrorists.

Because of the earthquake and tsunami in Japan and the damage to the Fukushima nuclear plant, German Chancellor Angela Merkel was one of the first leaders to take the initiative and decide to close the majority of the nuclear power plants in her country. This will amount to a costly act for Germany, nearly 1.4 billion dollars in initial estimates. The benefit that I can see from this is advancement towards alternative sources of energy.

Renewable sources of energy such as from the sun, wind, water, biomass and earth will benefit us and the future generations, plus they do not increase carbon dioxide levels and help in maintaining earth's temperature. Once Canada was forefront in the world in acquiring wind energy, which is, in fact, one of the fastest growing methods of generating electricity. It seems countries like Germany and Holland have overtaken this initiative with a lot of governmental support.

Canada, though, leads the world in solar collector development and commercialization. "In Canada, Photovoltaic technology has become the favored form of renewable energy technology due to a number of social and economical factors, including the need to reduce greenhouse gas."

Bioenergy is a renewable energy resource derived from living organisms and/or their by-products. It currently accounts for approximately 6% of Canada's total energy supply.

The other potential technologies available to us for harnessing energy are from wave, tidal and water currents.

Renewable energy technologies are one of the fastest growing energy markets in the world.

4. First Nations People

During my days in England, I had picked up a book called "Man's Rise to Civilization" by Peter Farb. I was shocked at how many different types of tribes existed in both North and South America and how different they were from each other. How some had excelled in their way of living by having double-storey houses while some lived in primitive shacks. The Hollywood cowboy movies had lumped them altogether as "Red Indians." Even though they were born here in Canada, my two sons never had an opportunity to intermingle with the First Nations people. Soon after my visit to the Mount Currie reservation (north of Whistler near Pemberton) and meeting members of the St'át'imc Nation, I invited a few of them to our place for dinner, making it possible for my children also to meet up with them. One of them had a very good sense of humor and asked me, "Which tribe are you from?" With a serious face I said, "I'm an Indian, from India, though I was born in Uganda." He persisted and said, "What tribe are you from?" I soon realized what he meant as his eyes travelled and landed on a photo of Darshana and me, wearing the Apache dress on Halloween day. We all had a big laugh and I jokingly blamed Darshana for dressing me up too. It was the third year in a row she had won first prize for her costume on Halloween day, while working at Royal Columbian Hospital.

Canada is the best country to live in but I couldn't boast about it anymore. For almost a decade (up to the year 2001), Canada was ranked number one among 175 countries in the United Nations' Quality of Life survey. Canada still manages to maintain a relatively high standard today. According to the 2004 UN Human Development Index, Canada was ranked fourth overall. Someone reminded me we were not number one any more. My ego was hurt. Is this due to the fact that we have not completely resolved the way we treat First Nations people?

The words of Peter Farb came to haunt me, "There is a great difficulty in finding a fitting word to describe the various peoples, mostly from Europe but also from parts of Asia, who came to the New World, made contact with the native inhabitants, and ultimately destroyed their cultures . . . a colonizer who early developed an advanced technology; he is an exploiter of human and natural resources; he has destroyed, often intentionally, almost every alien culture he has come in contact with; and he has imposed an iron rule on the remnant peoples of these cultures." We have come a long a way trying to build up trust and once again creating treaties but a reminder from the UN cautions us that we still have a long way to go.

5. Terry Fox

When the kids were in elementary school, every year they would have a "Terry Fox Run." I was very much touched by this humble soul, like plenty of others across this country. I would proudly post "Terry Fox Run" certificates in their bedrooms after completion of their run. In fact, they still have them well preserved and treasured in their own individual photo albums. Participating in the Terry Fox Run helped Milan to acquire the all-time record in school for the fastest 800 metre run, and that was for me the highlight of the elementary school years. Terry had discovered a malignant tumour in his right leg; the leg was amputated 15 centimetres above the knee. The night before his amputation he had read about an amputee runner and dreamed about running. On April 12, 1980 Terry dipped his artificial leg into the Atlantic Ocean and began his run, the "Marathon of Hope," across Canada, covering 43 kilometres a day and touching millions across the world with his painful wobble but having a sweet smile for thousands of well-wishers along the way. After 143 days and 5,373 kilometres, Terry stopped running as his primary cancer had spread to his lungs.

6. Animals

As Brew was getting old and very sick, we rushed him to the night clinic and the vet on duty recommended "to put him down." We took him home and the next day we took him to our family vet who also recommended the same. Finally, we took him to a special animal hospital and, after checking him out with a CT scan, a brain tumour was detected. The vet prescribed some medication to curtail the swelling of the tumour. The treatment cost us eight thousand dollars but gave Brew an extra eight months to live. This was exciting news for all, especially the kids. A friend at work remarked after hearing about the cost, "Prakash, I wouldn't even pay that much for some of my family members that I know of, to keep them alive." The idea was to make the kids realize that to take away life is easy but life is more precious.

7. Canadian Immigrants—Professionals

For the past thirty-five years, nothing has taken more of my time than the plight of foreign professionals, though the situation has improved in recent years. The story was the same, parents with their hard-earned money and a lot of personal sacrifice would put their children through colleges and universities and spend a lot more to send them abroad, to Canada, and coming here their dreams would be shattered. All their education would be wasted as their education and experience would not be recognized by the local institutes and work places would question them about their lack of Canadian experience. If Canadian Immigration required skilled labour then why are these skilled personnel doing menial jobs? The irony of the whole situation was that countries like India and China with their strong economies needed this skilled labour. I found a few cases where, after coming here and not finding a suitable job, they returned home and were hired by local companies who were ready to pay their return air fare. After hearing about my interview with the "Globe and Mail" regarding this situation, I was then invited to speak at the Conference Board of Canada and further stressed the need to address this issue. But it was not the time to wait for other institutes to take action. As I was a founding member of the Society of Punjabi Engineers and Technologists of BC, we took up the challenge ourselves to assist foreign-trained engineers and technicians to assist them in the form of career advice and job placement. The society is presently 500 members strong and is completely funded by the members. It assists professionals from various backgrounds and countries.

8. The Corporate World

This is a story about a friend who worked with an engineering firm that, during his time, through mergers and takeovers, grew to a company with over fifty thousand employees. This was a company that he was proud of and as they say, "gave up blood, sweat and tears." He worked honestly, worked hard and always had the best interests of the company at heart. The trouble started when a new manager was parachuted in from the east. The secretary quit within weeks of the manager taking on his new assignment, and made a complaint to Human Resources (HR). Soon after, the new secretary was fired by him. The receptionist quit too. All registered complains with HR. The new secretary was seen in tears one day after the manager had spoken to her. One senior technician was seen coming out of his office trembling and in shock. He had been working with the company for twenty years. Soon after, about ten technicians left for the same reason—the arrogance of one person. One of the most senior technologists quit too and was approached by the president of the company who asked him his reason for leaving. The answer was the same. A senior engineer also quit the company and the president approached him too. The reasons were the same. Finally, my hard-working friend couldn't take any more as, in the presence of others, the manager insulted him and belittled him. Several complaints went to HR and senior managers but all of them cast a blind eye. The fact that all who left are doing extremely well in their new positions speaks for itself, and even the newly hired engineers, one having a double honor degree and hoping to start his new career with this company, did not stay long and soon quit. They simply couldn't stand the manager and the company lost good potential employees. To this day the employees still wonder how the company took no action against a manager who had broken most of the rules of management and disrupted the lives of many, plus the fact that the company incurred heavy financial losses. Do HR personnel really have a say? More and more cases are heard of these managers who treat people with disrespect, often harassing and intimidating and creating a hostile environment, and I cannot believe in my country that we are breeding such managers. Once upon a time, as per the United Nations surveys, we were the most neutral and caring country in the world. We are slipping in the eyes of the world. Is this due to the global interaction and influence of some other dominating countries and their company culture where shareholders present themselves with heavy bonuses even though the firm is not making a profit and then file bankruptcy or ask governments to bail them out?

I remember the time that two of us senior technicians, Neil and I, were considered for an annual bonus though we were in the union. This was due to our dedicated extra effort and initiatives. Usually, the bonus was shared amongst supervisors, managers and engineers. When the time came for distribution, even though we had been promised, the general manager did not include us in the pool. Neil complained and we both received $500. I returned the cheque to the assistant manager saying, "In my culture we don't beg for the things which are promised to us." He took the cheque back. I had a weekend to think over my action. I went back to the manager next Monday morning and asked for the cheque back saying, "I'm going to share the cheque with the ten technicians and EITs (Engineers-in-Training), telling them the money was a Christmas gift from the company." The team really appreciated the kind gesture thinking it really came from the company. It wasn't more than a few months later that Neil, who had promised to keep the bonus issue a secret, shared the truth with the team. So often we see signs posted by companies "Employees come first" or "Employees/People make the company." There is genuine joy in sharing and hopefully more of us can appreciate that feeling.

9. Sports—From Cricket to Canucks

In 2010 my personal dream of having an Indian cricket club was realized and the IndCan Cricket Club was included among the thirty-odd clubs and seventy teams participating in the British Columbia Mainland Cricket League. It was a pleasure working with Burnaby Parks Board as they considered our request for a new ground and a new pitch which was long overdue and cost about twenty thousand dollars. Cricket was special to me as my father and his brother had done well in that sport; it had helped them with their careers and they also credited their good health in later years to this sport.

But my sons, who were born in this country and all grown up now, never let me forget that this is my new home now and, even though I love cricket, they're completely amused when I jump up with excitement whenever our home hockey team "Canucks" scores a goal. More so now, as the team, for the first time in eighteen years, is in the finals and has the opportunity to win the prestigious "Stanley Cup."

10. Roots

It had been my long-term desire to show my sons, who had never been to India, the country where their forefathers had originally come from. It was the right time and with the help of Darshana we planned a trip. The economy was booming and our relations in India were all doing quite well. Ronak had always wanted to go by himself but I had convinced him to be patient and make a trip together. They were sick of hearing about the country that I had always praised and they now also heard it from their mother. Darshana was one patriotic lady, would take you to task if you even dared to say anything negative about the country of her birth. The kids were determined to prove us wrong somehow, even jokingly, for trying to brainwash them, which was never the case but rather the love for its culture, family values, food, music, art, dance, spirituality, architecture, hospitality, and democratic values were all precious to both of us.

Whether it was the boat ride from the southernmost point of India to the Vivekananda Rock Memorial, or the train ride from Goa to Mumbai, or staying and journeying around the back waters of Kerala in a houseboat, all were memorable times to treasure. They enjoyed the elephant rides in Jaipur and the horse rides on Mount Abu and the camel rides in the desert city of Jaisalmer. Swimming in the Indian Ocean, parasailing or just lying on the beach took a lot of stress away. There were lots of old castles with fascinating stories, which the guide made sure Ronak and Milan understood as he tried his best to detail its history in English. As most of the places we visited were by car with a hired driver, it was easy to pull over and stop at a hotel and rest for the night. Milan made the mistake of visiting an Indian ground toilet instead of the English toilet with a seat. Not having seen one before he said to himself, "Oh! Still under construction!" He went to the next one and said the same thing. Finally he came back and we all burst out laughing. Soon he found one that he was used to. They couldn't stop taking photos at Agra, seeing the magnificent Taj Mahal. The temples of South India were spectacular; just to name a few, the Meenakshi Temple at Madurai, the Rameshwaram Temple at the east coastal city of Rameshwaram on the Bay of Bengal and the Temple of Lord Venkateshwara at Tirupati.

They finally met their distant cousins, two sisters and a brother, in Vadodara. They had never met before and to their surprise the sisters (Sneha and Nandini) had brought each one a bouquet of flowers and offered them a ride on their scooters. This is not what the brothers had ever imagined. While my nephew (Dwarkesh) drove us home in the Indian Jeep, the brothers followed on scooters holding onto the flowers, quite shocked—the scene was fit for a movie.

My favourite place was visiting the Gandhi Ashram in the city of Ahmedabad located on the shores of the Sabarmati River. Ronak and Milan could feel the excitement I was undergoing and teased me about it. It was formerly called "Satyagraha Ashram." (The ashram was started in all earnest with a two-fold purpose, one was to carry on the search for truth and the other was to create a non-violent group of workers, who would organize and help to secure freedom for the country. While at Sabarmati, Gandhiji lived in a small cottage, which is now known as "Hridaya (heart) kunj". It is a place of great historic value, where even today visitors find some of the things that Gandhiji used—a writing desk, a khadi kurta, a yarn spun by him and some letters.) This was the highlight of my trip to India.

11. Home

Henry Kyemba was a former Minister in the Amin government (1972-1977), Vice President of the World Health Organization and chairman of the African Health Ministers. He knew Idi Amin for 20 years. A graduate of Makerere University and from 1969 to 1979 he was principal private secretary to Uganda's President Dr. Milton Obote. He fled in May 1977. His book "State of Blood" gave a thorough account of Idi Amin's atrocities in Uganda. In order to secure his regime, Amin launched a campaign of persecution against rival tribes and Obote supporters, murdering between 100,000 and 500,000 (most sources say 300,000).

Among those to die were ordinary citizens, former and serving cabinet ministers, the Chief Justice, Supreme Court judges, diplomats, academics, educators, prominent Roman Catholic and Anglican clergy, senior bureaucrats, medical practitioners, bankers, tribal leaders, business executives, journalists and a number of foreigners. In some cases, entire villages were wiped out. So many corpses were thrown into the River Nile that workers at one location had to continuously fish them out to stop the intake ducts at a nearby dam from becoming clogged.

Henry Kyemba described Amin's women, his insatiable appetite, the dismembered body of his wife Kay, the bizarre tale of five wives, more than thirty children and more than thirty mistresses. He also described Amin's private visits to the morgue and the gruesome tastes he had personally described to Kyemba.

Amin expelled everyone of Indian origin, eighty thousand-plus Indians and Pakistanis in 1972. On Friday August 5th, 1972, while in Soroti, Amin had a dream in which, he says, God informed him to get rid of British citizens, mainly Indians, Pakistanis, etc. The following Monday, in the Parliament, he announced and signed a decree to "get rid of the so-called foreigners." This action was initiated by Amin and without any consultation with his Cabinet Ministers. They were shocked by this action too. The Asians, including third generation descendants, were given 90 days to leave the country and were only allowed to take what they could carry. "If they do not leave they will find themselves on fire," Amin warned.

Living in Vancouver, British Columbia we heard the news that all of us Asians had longed to hear for so long. On 11th April 1979, Julius Nyerere's Tanzanian army, beating back Ugandan's heavy resistance, had taken control of Kampala. Amin with his family, four wives, several of his thirty mistresses and about twenty of his children fled to Libya and then finally settled in Saudi Arabia.

President Museveni was involved in the war that deposed Idi Amin. He is a politician and a statesman. He has been President of Uganda since 26th January 1986. With the notable exception of northern areas, Museveni has brought relative stability and economic growth to a country that has endured decades of government mismanagement, rebel activity and civil war. His tenure has also witnessed one of the most effective national responses to HIV/AIDS in Africa. He personally travelled to places like Britain where most of the Ugandan Asian refugees had settled encouraging them to come back to Uganda and reinvest. In the mid-to-late 1990s he was lauded by the west as part of a new generation of African leaders. Recent developments, including the abolition of presidential term limits before the 2006 elections and the harassment of democratic opposition, have attracted concern from domestic commentators and the international community.

In a newscast from Uganda during the recent elections there in April 2011, a senior Ugandan judge said, "If Museveni of 1984 were to meet Museveni of 2011, he would shoot him." He was referring to the time when in the 1980s Museveni condemned African leaders for hanging onto power for too long.

But this is my new home now, Canada, and the concerns that I have raised are genuine ones as I wish to see my country prosper and internationally deserve the praises it once was showered with. All of the above concerns which I have addressed, plus the plight of the poor and homeless, need to be given top priority. As for my part, I wish that I and my community of the newly arrived immigrants to this part of the world will live and contribute like the Parsi Community did in India.

Parsi or Parsee refers to a member of the larger of the two Persian Zoroastrian communities in South Asia, the other being the Irani community. According to tradition, the present-day Parsis descend from a group of Persian Zoroastrians who immigrated to India during the 10th Century AD due to the persecution by Muslims in Greater Persia. They first landed in Gujarat. The Parsis have made considerable contributions to the history and development of India, considering their small numbers.

Chief Minister Narendra Modi, while speaking at Parsi pilgrim place Udvada on the 1290th birth celebration of Parsi Atash Behram, said, "This is the community that doesn't want anything from the government. They didn't even want election ticket. This shows that their love is without condition, without any expectation. I haven't heard of any Parsi going to jail. All other communities have tasted jail term, but not Parsis. Some tradition, some 'Samskar' must be there to make this possible, and Gujarat is benefited by it. One would find Parsi on the top of every area, be it industry, science, army or any other area. It is fact that Parsis didn't increase population, but I think if Parsis had done it, the nation could get great benefit out of it, and I pray Iranshah for more contribution of Parsis to this nation."

Shri Modi added he is indebted to the Parsi community and that he seeks the blessings of **"Humata-Hukhta-Huvarshta" (Good thoughts-good words-good deeds).**

Dehli (Bahá'í Temple)

Agra (Taj Mahal)

Jaipur (Hawa Mahal)

Jaisalmer, Rajasthan

Mount Abu

*Ahmedabad, Gujarat Gandhi
Ashram / Sabarmati River*

Vadodara, Gujarat

Kamati Baug (Park)

Yamuna Trading "Agarbatti" shop (Owner-Rajen Mehta)
Mumbai, Maharashtra

*Taj Hotel Bangalore,
Karnataka*

*Parliament Building
Mysore, Karnataka*

Mysore Palace

Madurai, Tamil Nadu

Rameshwaram, Tamil Nadu

Rameshwaram Temple

Kanyakumari, Southernmost point in India, Tamil Nadu.

Swami Vivekananda Rock Memorial
Kerala State

Houseboat

Family and Friends – Later Years of Fond memories in photos

Milan, Aaliyah and Vega Joshi

Prakesh and papa Vinod Joshi

Dipan and Pratiksha Vyas / Darshana and Prakash Vora in Mumbai India-2023

Darshana at her Chembur, Mumbai House August 2023

Rohan, Tejaswini and Nikhil

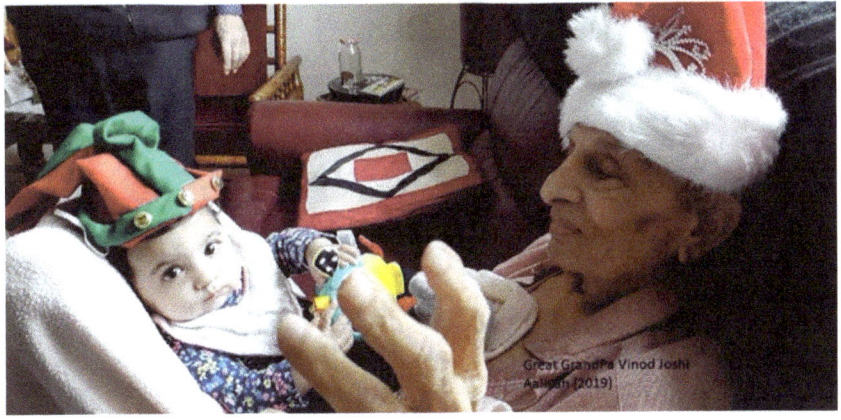

Great GrandPa Vinod Joshi
Aaliyah (2019)

Tushar Patel

Indu & Vinod Joshi/Milan & Vega Joshi/Prakash & Darshana Joshi/Louise & Debbie D' Mello
(June 2nd 2017)

Celebrating my 70th Birthday.
(October 10, 2020) at Sechelt, BC, Canada

Chichen Itza, Mexico (January 2024)

Amaya with Kirby

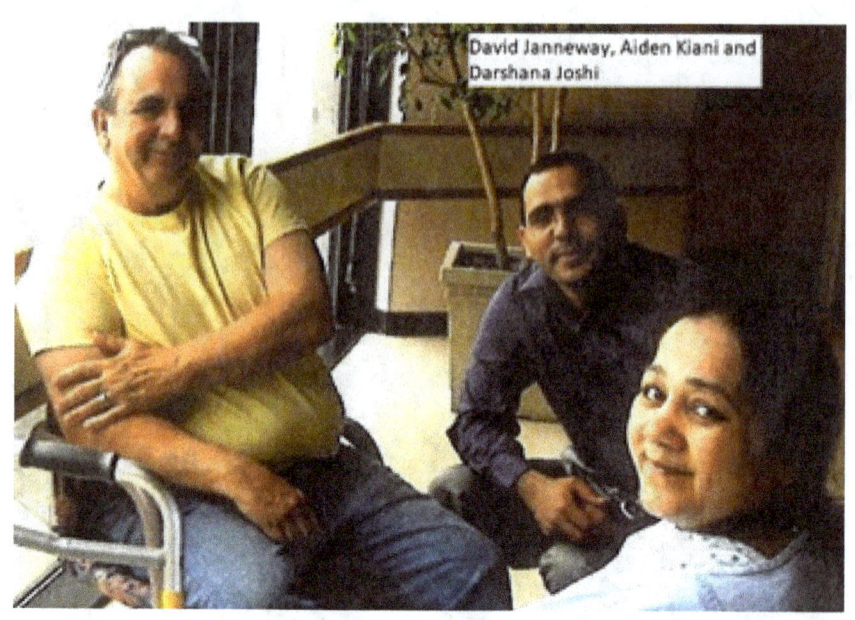
David Janneway, Aiden Kiani and Darshana Joshi

Work History in Photos

Metro Testing & Engineering (April 2024)

My First Boss in Canada - Harry Watson
Hardy Associates, 1976

Hardy Associates (1975), Sam Watanabe, Rupert Sankar, Prakash Joshi, Salim Faruq

Hardy & Associates (1978) 2014 Reunion

Ross Retie / Geff Groombridge / Barry Watson   Ed Harrington

First Full-Time Job, Teacher Grade 6/7 (1970), Masaka, Uganda

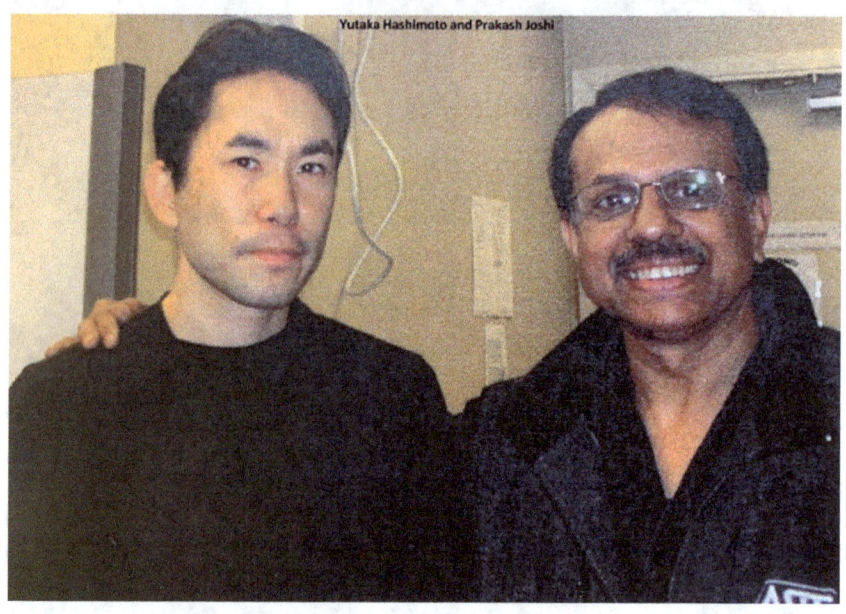
Yutaka Hashimoto and Prakash Joshi

Prakash Joshi with Jay Drew, P.Eng., founder of Lock Block Company and also inventor of Lock Blocks (stacked in the background) with intent to save and recycle left-over ready mix concrete During his involvement with Tetra Society Chapter in Vancouver, Jay has created dozens of devices to help the disabled lead easier and more self-sufficient lives

Volunteer Work

CERTIFICATE OF RECOGNITION

PRESENTED TO

Prakash Vinodrai Joshi, P.L.Eng.

IN APPRECIATION OF YOUR VOLUNTEER CONTRIBUTION
ON THE FOLLOWING GROUPS OR COMMITTEES:

Mentoring Program

JULY 1, 2022 - JUNE 30, 2023

PRAKASH JOSHI
AScT, PTech, PLEng

Prakash is a materials technologist with experience working in the construction industry. After nearly 30 years with Amec Earth & Environmental Limited, Prakash joined Metro Testing Ltd. where he works as a senior materials engineering technologist. He has served on the ASTTBC Board since 2022, and is also a member of the Appeals Board, past member of the ASTTBC Awards Committee, designate mentor for EGBC, past-president of the Society of Punjabi Engineers and Technicians of BC, past vice-president of the Uganda-Canadian National Association (UCNA), as well as past BC regional coordinator of "Initiatives of Change". He has been a keynote speaker at various events including BCIT Career Nights. Prakash is a composer, musician, singer, and author of 'Life in Four Continents'.

ASTTBC – Meetings held at Indian Educational Institutes

New Dehli
1. Ministry of Human Resources Development
2. National Institutes of Technology
3. Canadian Immigrant Integration Program
4. Trade and Investment in British Technology
5. National Skill Development Corporation
6. IIT, Dehli

Noida:
1. Amity University
2. All India Council for Technical Education
3. Institute of Engineers of India (IEI)

Mumbai:
1. IIT, Powai, Mumbai
2. Maharashtra Education Board (Directorate of Technical Education)
3. Thakur University

Pune:
1. MIT Skills, (Pune University)
2. University of Kalyani

(Days off: visited Bahaii Temple and Swami Narayan Akshardham)

ASTTBC (Applied Science Technologists and Technicians of BC-2024)-Director

CANFACS (Canada Nepal Friendship and Cultural Society)-Director

EGBC (Engineers and Geoscientists of BC) – Designate Mentor

SPEATBC (Society of Punjabi Engineers and Technicians of BC) –Past Presidents Council

Music- Special Fond Memories

Prakash Joshi with Guruji Devinder Hu... - Kala Mandir

Home Music Room
at 1645 Ellesmere Avenue
Burnaby, BC
Canada

Cricket – (IndCan Cricket Club of BC)

IndCan Cricket Club dinner (2022)

Cricket club at Kensington Ground, Burnaby, BC, Canada

B. S. Chandrasekhar, top echelon of leg spinner at Stanely Park, Vancouver after a friendly game. (1980's)

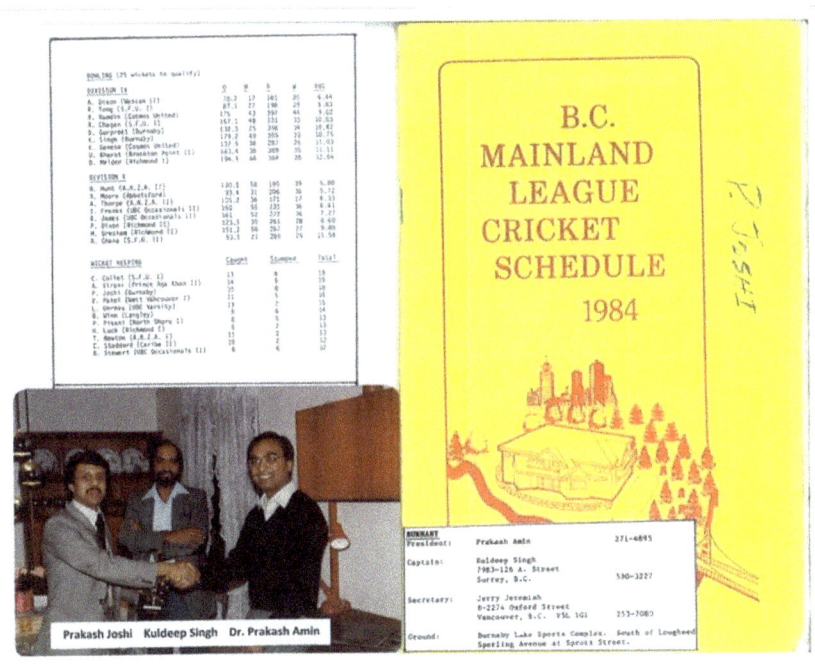

www.ingramcontent.com/pod-product-compliance
Lightning Source LLC
LaVergne TN
LVHW012245070526
838201LV00090B/124